The Scottish Terrier

– A Complete Anthology of the Dog –

1850-1940

ISBN No.
978-14455-2653-9 (Paperback)
978-14455-2773-4 (Hardback)

British Library Cataloguing-in-Publication Data
A catalogue record for this book is available from
the British Library

VDB

www.vintagedogbooks.com

Contents

Containing chapters from the following sources:

Of noxious vermin rids the house and store :
Inspects each corner, searches every floor.

SCOTCH TERRIER.

THE SCOTCH TERRIER

Is a shorter-legged, and generally a heavier dog than either of the preceding varieties. He is equally plucky and clever, but not so active, and from this, and his thicker coat, is not so serviceable in hunting rabbits.

His *hair* is long and matted, and often soft and silky. His *colour* is usually a rich black and tan, sometimes mixed with dark grey ; it is impossible to look at his coat and colour and not suspect a cross with the Colley. In *height* he is seldom over 14 inches, but sometimes weighs more than 16 or 18 lbs. There are innumerable varieties of this breed.

THE SCOTCH TERRIER,

A small rough terrier under the above name has for many years been known in England, and accepted by the inhabitants of that country as identical with the true breed as recognised in Scotland. Within the last few years, however, our northern fellow-countrymen have come forward and repudiated him, alleging that he is not the genuine article; and in their Scottish dog shows they have produced specimens of what they consider the pure breed, including the originals of the engraving which accompanies this article.

On comparing these dogs with Mr. Radclyffe's Rough (one of the group of terriers in the frontispiece of Book III.), it will be seen that they closely resemble him; and very probably Mr. Radclyffe obtained his breed from the north, as it was one not generally met with in Wales, where that gentleman lived. In any case, however, it is admitted that the Scotch dog as described below, with the sanction of nearly every well-known breeder of the present day, is of great antiquity, and it must not be confounded with the over-sized, long-backed dogs with large and heavily-feathered ears, whose traces of Skye ancestry are evident to those who understand the two breeds from which they spring. In fact, it is in the ears that one of the chief characteristics of the Scotch terrier lies, for all unite in agreeing that they should be small, and covered with a velvety coat—not large, and fringed with hair like a prick-haired Skye terrier. As regards the carriage of the ear, the opinions of those best qualified to judge are a little divided between the merits of a perfectly erect and half-drop ear; but all unite in their condemnation of a perfectly drop, button, or fox-terrier ear; which stands erect, but falls over at the tip, half covering the orifice, a large, very large, majority of modern breeders agree in preferring the small, erect, sharp-pointed one; though all would probably hesitate to pass over a really good terrier who had half-prick ears. Another great feature in the Scotch terrier is his coat, which should be intensely hard and wiry, and not too long, and is well described in the appended scale of points, which bears the signatures of nearly all the leading breeders.

As a dead-game animal, the Scotch terrier is not to be surpassed by any breed except bulls or bull terriers, but the courage of the latter dogs is so exceptional that it is no disrespect to any other dog to place them for pluck in a class by themselves, and, pound for pound, there is no dog, but a bull terrier, who can beat the hard-haired Scotchman by far. Still, he has a natural advantage over the bull terrier, for his hard coat and thickly padded feet enable him to go through whins and over rocky places where the other would be useless, and he is far more easy to control, though naturally of a rather pugnacious disposition. His intelligence and love of home, his pluck, docility, and affection for his master, should make Scottie a favourite with all who want a varmint dog; and nobody who once gets a good one, of the right style and stamp, will care to let him go.

The dogs selected for illustration are Miss Mary Laing's Foxie, by Sharp—Fan, bred by Mr. John L. Grainger, of Aberdeen; and Mr. J. A. Adamson's Roger Rough, by Fury—Flo, by Mr. Cattanack's Don—Mr. J. L. Grainger's Nelly. This

4

SCOTCH TERRIERS.—MISS MARY LAING'S "FOXIE" AND MR. J. A. ADAMSON'S "ROGER ROUGH."

dog was bred by Mr. A. Barclay in 1876. The former is a very grand-bodied dog, and his head is good, though his ears are on the big side. Roger Rough, on the contrary, excels in head properties; but both are very typical specimens of the breed. Foxie has won first prizes at Edinburgh, Aberdeen, Montrose, and Kilmarnock; whilst his old opponent Roger Rough has been successful at the Crystal Palace (twice), Aberdeen, Edinburgh, Ayr, &c., though he was passed over at the Alexandra Palace of December, 1881, for a supposed, but purely imaginary, want of terrier character.

Amongst other good dogs Messrs. Blomfield and Ludlow's Bon Accord and Splinter II. may be favourably noticed; but it must be remembered that many excellent specimens are seldom exhibited, or only appear at Highland shows, where their merits are hidden from the public gaze.

The following is the scale of points which has been submitted to the chief breeders of this terrier, and approved of by them in the document appended to this article.

POINTS OF THE HARD-HAIRED SCOTCH TERRIER.

	Value.		Value.		Value.
Skull	5	Neck	5	Coat	20
Muzzle	5	Chest	5	Size	10
Eyes	5	Body	10	Colour	2½
Ears	10	Legs and feet	10	General appearance	10
		Tail	2½		
	25		32½		42½

Grand Total 100.

Skull (value 5) proportionately long, slightly domed, and covered with short hard hair about ¾in. long, or less. It should not be quite flat, as there should be a sort of stop, or drop, between the eyes.

Muzzle (value 5) very powerful, and gradually tapering towards the nose, which should always be black and of a good size. The jaws should be perfectly level and the teeth square, though the nose projects somewhat over the mouth, which gives the impression of the upper jaw being longer than the under one.

Eyes (value 5) set wide apart, of a dark brown or hazel colour; small, piercing, very bright, and rather sunken.

Ears (value 10) very small, prick or half-prick (the former is preferable), but never drop. They should also be sharp-pointed, and the hair on them should not be long, but velvety, and they should not be cut. The ears should be free from any fringe at the top.

Neck (value 5) short, thick and muscular; strongly set on sloping shoulders.

Chest (value 5) broad in comparison to the size of the dog, and proportionately deep.

Body (value 10) of moderate length, not so long as a Skye's, and rather flat-sided; but well ribbed up, and exceedingly strong in hind quarters.

Legs and Feet (value 10), both fore and hind legs, should be short, and very heavy in bone, the former being straight, or slightly bent, and well set on under the

6

body as the Scotch terrier should not be out at elbows. The hocks should be bent, and the thighs very muscular; and the feet strong, small, and thickly covered with short hair, the fore feet being larger than the hind ones, and well let down on the ground.

The Tail (value 2¼), which is never cut, should be about 7in. long, carried with a slight bend, and often gaily.

The Coat (value 20) should be rather short (about 2in.), intensely hard and wiry in texture, and very dense all over the body.

Size (value 10) about 14lb. to 18lb. for a dog, 13lb. to 17lb. for a bitch.

Colours (value 2½) steel or iron grey, brindle, black, red, wheaten, and even yellow or mustard colour. It may be observed that mustard, black, and red are not usually so popular as the other colours. White markings are most objectionable.

General Appearance (value 10).—The face should wear a very sharp, bright, and active expression, and the head should be carried up. The dog (owing to the shortness of his coat) should appear to be higher on the leg than he really is; but, at the same time, he should look compact, and possessed of great muscle in his hind-quarters. In fact, a Scotch terrier, though essentially a terrier, cannot be too powerfully put together. He should be from about 9in. to 12in. in height, and should have the appearance of being higher on the hind legs than on the fore.

FAULTS.

Muzzle either under or over-hung.

Eyes large or light-coloured.

Ears large, round at the points, or drop. It is also a fault if they are too heavily covered with hair.

Coat.—Any silkiness, wave, or tendency to curl is a serious blemish, as is also an open coat.

Size.—Specimens over 18lb. should not be encouraged.

Having read the above standard, and considered the same, I am prepared to express my approval of it, and will give it my support when breeding or judging hard-haired Scotch terriers.

DAVID ADAMS, Murrygate, Dundee.
J. A. ADAMSON, Ashley-road, Aberdeen.
ALEX. BARCLAY, Springbank-terrace, Aberdeen.
H. BLOMFIELD, Lakenham, Norfolk.
JAMES BURR, M.D., Aberdeen.
J. C. CARRICK, Carlisle.
JOHN CUMMING, Bridge of Don, Aberdeen.
W. D. FINDLAY, Portlethen, Aberdeenshire.
WM. FRAZER, Jasmine-terrace, Aberdeen.
JOHN L. GRAINGER, Summer-street, Aberdeen.
D. J. THOMPSON GRAY, South George-street, Dundee.
PAT HENDERSON, Tally-street, Dundee.
MARY LAING, Granton Lodge, Aberdeen.
P. R. LATHAM, Tweed-terrace, Bridge of Allan.
H. J. LUDLOW, St. Giles Plain, Norwich.

JAMES D. LUMSDEN, Pitcairnfield, Perth.
JOHN D. M'COLL, Burnfoot, Cardross.
JAMES M'LAREN, Blarhullachen, Aberfoyle.
WM. MEFF, JUN., Market-street, Aberdeen.
J. R. MONKMAN, Pitmuxton, Aberdeen.
JAMES B. MORRISON, Brookfield, Greenock.
JOHN PIRIE, Clarence-road, Wood Green.
GEO. ROBERTSON, Salisbury-terrace, Aberdeen.
VERO SHAW, London.
A. STEPHEN, Frazerburgh.
ALEX. SUTHERLAND, Aberdeen.
ALEX. THOMSON, Bromshill Lodge, Aberdeen.
GEORGE THOMPSON, Powis Lodge, Aberdeen.
PAT. C. THOMSON, Milnacraig, Alyth.
DAVID N. WALLACE, Skene-row, Aberdeen.
W. B. WIGHT, Dyce, Aberdeenshire.

7

THE SCOTCH TERRIER.

THIS interesting breed of dog is supposed by very many of its admirers to have been the progenitor of the Irish Terrier, and is considered by them to have been introduced into the sister isle by emigrants from Scotland, who were accompanied to so their new residence by their faithful canine companions, who were destined to found the race of Irish Terriers. That there is ground for this impression we willingly admit, and as the head in certain characteristics approaches the Irish Terrier, we pass from one to the other, so that our readers may have a fair opportunity of comparing the two varieties. As the Scotch Terrier is so little known in the southern portion of these islands, and a class for this variety is a very uncommon institution at any shows, we consider ourselves fortunate in being able to lay the views of Mr. James B. Morrison before our readers. This gentleman has on several occasions judged the Scotch Terrier, and his knowledge of and connection with the breed has extended over several years. Mr. Morrison writes :—

"Every dog has his day, and, thanks to the continued efforts of a few admirers of the Hard-haired Scotch Terrier, there is every likelihood of 'Scottie' being better known and more appreciated, both by authorities on canine affairs and the public generally, than he has been since the advent of dog-shows.

"The designation *hard-haired* Scotch Terrier implies the existence of softer haired varieties, and these we find in the Skye and Dandie Dinmont. Fanciers of these two terriers can, no doubt, recognise their favourites in fusty books of 'ye olden time;' and without denying them the satisfaction of an inconceivable antiquity, it requires no great stretch of imagination to suppose, that at a time considerably posterior to the Cambrian period, the three varieties mentioned might have appeared under our present heading, having had a common origin, just as the short hard-haired, and longer and softer coated, together with the bob-tailed variety of Sheep-dog, are believed to have sprung from the same stock.

"It is more than likely that the subject of this chapter was the original Terrier of Scotland, from the fact that the hard, short coat could not have been produced from the Skye or any other longer haired variety, without the presence of a smooth-coated dog ; and we know that, with the exception of the Blue Paul—a dog about forty-five pounds weight, bred at Kirkintilloch, which has come and almost gone within the last century and a half—there was no smooth-coated species indigenous to the Highlands, or Islands of Scotland, or even known to Lowlanders as a Scotch dog. It may be advanced that the hard, short coat is the result of judicious selection, but against this theory stands the fact, that in the Scotch Terrier era these dogs were used exclusively for work, and the great object in breeding was to produce an intelligent, plucky terrier, of a useful size, with a long powerful jaw, broad deep chest, and strong loins ; colour, length of coat, carriage, &c., being secondary considerations—a course followed in certain quarters to this day. Such a

8

specimen as 'The Shipwrecked Poodle,' which has become quite historical in the canine world, and who was blamed for the introduction of the silky-coated Skye, might, on the other hand, if crossed with the Scotch Terrier, produce a dog not unlike the modern Skye.

"In ferreting out the origin of the Scotch Terrier, we are reminded of the greater antiquity claimed for an inventive Scion of the Macleods for his clan over the Macgregors. Macgregor approached the ante-diluvian period as nearly as the Macleods' credulity, and his own connection with the Auld Kirk would permit; however, his opponent settled the matter to his own satisfaction at least, with the query, 'Did you'll ever know a Macleod that had not a poat of her own?' Whether or not the Macleod saved from the wreck of nature a brace of Scotch Terriers in 'her poat,' is 'not proven,' but they were known, and better known than they are to-day, at a time when we were indebted to ballad-singers for rescuing our own history from oblivion. The best Scotch Terrier authorities of our day are the more veteran of our Highland crofters and keepers, men who, unfortunately, wei *compelled* to keep these terriers for the extermination of vermin, or, at least, to enable them to hold their own. We learn from this source that they were found in considerable numbers all over the islands and the mainland in the North-west of Scotland in the beginning of the present century.

"This is a terrier peculiarly adapted for the work cut out for him, in unearthing such vermin as the fox, otter, badger, wild cat, &c., than which the gamekeeper and farmer have not more indefatigable poachers to contend against.

"Dealing with such ticklish customers in their strongholds among the rocks, boulders, and cairns, or burrows, is no light task, but in the Scotch Terrier we have the assistance of an able and ever-willing ally, who, having a remarkable nose, gives tongue at once on the scent, following it up to the lair with spirit, where he works silently in on belly or side, if need be, till close upon the enemy, when outsiders can hear that the real work has begun.

"When he has heavy mettle to deal with, unless assisted by a pack, who rarely allow the foe to die from home, he compels the varmint to bolt for a reckoning outside; if the struggle is severe or protracted, the terrier who has borne the brunt may be seen coming panting to the open air for breathing space, bringing with him evidence of the severity of the combat; however, the sounds of war are too much for him, and indifferent to the kindly attentions of his master, he returns to the charge the embodiment of determination and excitement.

"Many a gallant little dog has found his grave in the maze of these cairns, the result of the encounter in many cases turning out to be a Cadmean victory, where a terrier either loses himself in the labyrinth of passages and crannies, or jumps over the ledge of a rock which he cannot ascend again, when he is entirely out of his master's reach. In some instances food can be thrown in to him from day to day until the boulders are removed or blasted, but this is not always practicable; if in a burrow, a few hours may suffice to dig him out if within call at all, although numbers are buried alive, paying for their temerity with their life.

"Working dogs are best studied in the field, being out of their element at the end of a yard and a half of chain on a show-bench; and a day spent on the Highlands with a keeper and his gang of terriers is fraught with interest and instruction to an admirer of the hardy tyke.

"When off duty—unlike the shambling drawing-room terrier out for an airing—he is sprightly, vigorous and gay, full of life and activity, the slightest attention paid him occasioning the most demonstrative delight; no day is too long for him; he is naturally mild-tempered and under ordinary circumstances not quarrelsome, although able to hold his own in an 'emergency;' he is a wonderful follower, even in puppyhood, a very valuable qualification when introduced to city life.

"The comparative scarcity of vermin in the Highlands shows how effectually the Scotch Terrier has done his work, and the recent neglect of this hardy little mountaineer may be attributed to the very fact that he has in a great measure outlived his occupation.

"While advocating the judging of working dogs by their performances in the field principally, it is necessary to erect a general standard of excellence for awards in the ring, and this can best be arrived at by a careful study of the points necessary to enable each breed to fill in the most efficient manner the sphere it has to occupy. I give the following description of the general appearance and points of the Hard-haired Scotch Terrier from dogs acknowledged to be good specimens by veteran breeders, whose testimony being the outcome of personal experience is entitled to be considered of the highest value; these points have also been adopted by the present generation of Scotch Terrier fanciers as correct:—

POINTS OF THE SCOTCH TERRIER.

"The *General Appearance* is that of a thick-set, compact, short-coated terrier, standing about 9½ inches high, with body long in comparison, and averaging 16lbs. or 17lbs. weight for dogs, and 2lbs. less for bitches; with ears and tail uncut. Although in reality no higher at shoulder than the Skye or Dandie Dinmont, it has a leggier appearance, from the fact that the coat is much shorter than in these two varieties. The head is carried pretty high, showing an intelligent, cheery face.

"The *Temperament.*—An incessant restlessness and perpetual motion, accompanied by an eager look, asking plainly for the word of command; a muscular form, fitting him for the most arduous work; and sagacity, intelligence, and courage to make the most of the situation, qualify the Scotch Terrier for the rôle of 'friend of the family,' or 'companion in arms'—*amicus humani generis*—in a sense unsurpassed by any other dog, large or small.

"The *Head* is longish and bold rather than round, and is full between the eyes; it is free from long, soft, or woolly hair, or top-knot, and is smaller in the bitch than in the dog.

"The *Muzzle* is a most important point, and should be long and very powerful, tapering slightly to the nose, which should be well formed, well spread over the muzzle, and invariably black; there must be no approach to snipishness; the teeth should be perfectly level in front, neither being under or over shot, canines fitting well together. A mouth off the level should not altogether disqualify, as this fault is often met with in the very best blood; however, it must always be considered very objectionable. The roof of the mouth is almost invariably black.

"The *Eyes* are very small, well sunk in the head, dark hazel, bright and expressive, with heavy eyebrows.

"The *Ears* are very small and free from long hair, feather, or fringe; in fact, as a rule, rather bare of hair; they are either carried erect, or semi-erect, the latter preferred for a workman—never drop-eared and never cut.

10

" The *Neck* is short, thick, and very muscular, well set between the shoulders, and showing great power.

" The *Chest* and *Body*.—The body gives an impression of great strength, being a combination of little else than bone and muscle. The chest is broad and deep; the ribs flat —a wonderful provision of nature, indispensable to a dog often compelled to force its way into burrows and dens on its side; the back broad; the loins broad and very strong; this is a feature calling for special attention, as a dog in any degree weak in the hind quarters lacks one of the main points in this breed, and should on no account be used as a stud dog. The body is covered with a dense, hard, wet-resisting coat about two inches long.

" The *Legs*.—Fore legs are short and straight, with immense bone for a dog of this size; elbows in same plane as shoulder-joints and not outside, the forearm being particularly muscular; the hind legs are also strong, the thighs being well developed and thick, the hocks well bent and never straight. The feet are small and firmly padded to resist the stony, broken ground, with strong nails generally black. Although free from feathering, the legs and feet are well covered with hair to the very toes.

" The *Tail* should not exceed 7 or 8 inches; it is covered with the same quality and length of hair as the body, is carried with a slight bend, and should not be docked.

" The *Colour* is various shades of grey, or grizzle and brindle, the most desirable colour being red brindle with black muzzle and ear-tips."

From the above it appears that the Scotch Terrier, like his Irish relative, may be reckoned "dead game;" his temperament, however, is more vivacious than the somewhat stolid Irishman. Mr. Morrison has so thoroughly described the variety that we consider further remarks on the points unnecessary, and therefore adopt the above as a true description of the breed, merely giving a table by which the variety can be judged.

SCALE OF POINTS FOR JUDGING SCOTCH TERRIERS.

Skull, shape, &c.	5
Muzzle and teeth	10
Eyes and ears	5
Neck	5
Body	5
Feet and legs	5
Coat	10
General appearance, temper	5
	50

THE SCOTTISH TERRIER.

FROM all I have been told, and from what I have read, I believe that this little dog is the oldest variety of the canine race indigenous to North Britain, although but a comparatively recent introduction across the border and into fashionable society, at any rate under his present name. For generations he had been a popular dog in the Highlands, where, strangely enough, he was always known as the Skye terrier, although he is so different from the long-coated, unsporting-like looking creature with which that name is now associated. Even Hugh Dalziel, in the first edition of his "British Dogs," published so recently as 1881, gives an excellent illustration of the Scotch terrier which he calls a Skye terrier.

Our little friend has, perhaps, been rather unfortunate so far as nomenclature is concerned, for, after being called a Skye terrier, he became known as the Scotch terrier, the Scots terrier, and the

Highland terrier; then others dubbed him the Cairn terrier and the Die Hard, whilst another move was made to give him the distinguishing appellation of the Aberdeen terrier. Now he has been thoroughly wound up, and, I suppose to suit those persons of teetotal proclivities who connected the word " Scotch " with the national liquor called whiskey, has developed into the " Scottish " terrier; as such he is known in the Stud Books, and is acknowledged as of that name by the leading Scotch, or Scottish, authorities on the variety. Well, he is a game, smart, perky little terrier, and I do not think that his general excellence and desirability as a companion are likely to suffer from the evolutions his name has undergone. Years ago, before dog shows were invented, any cross bred creature was called a Scotch terrier, especially if he appeared to stand rather higher on the legs than the ordinary terrier; if he were on short legs he was an " otter " terrier.

In an old " Sportsman," a three halfpenny little magazine published in 1833, there is a wood engraving, by no means a bad one, of " The Scotch terrier." This is a big, leggy, cut-eared dog with a docked tail, evidently hard in coat and very game looking; were such a dog to be shown to-day he would be most likely to take a prize in the Irish terrier classes. The letterpress description does not, however, tally with the picture, for after saying that the Scotch terrier is purest in point of breed, it proceeds to state that "the Scotch terrier is generally low in stature, seldom more than 12in. or 14in. in height, with a strong muscular body and stout legs; his ears small and half pricked; his head is rather large in proportion to the size of his body, and his muzzle is considerably pointed. His scent is extremely acute, so that he can trace the footsteps of other animals with certainty; he is generally of a sand colour or black, dogs of this colour being certainly the most hardy and most to be depended upon. When white or pied, it is a sure mark of the impurity of the breed. The hair of this terrier is long, matted, and hard over almost every part of his body. His bite is extremely keen." This is not a bad description of a Scottish terrier of the present day, excepting that the matted coat is not required, that the semi-erect ears are not fashionable, and that a white specimen of pure blood crops up occasionally.

However, the same writer goes on to state that "there are three distinct varieties of the Scotch terrier, viz., the one above described; another about the same size as the former, but with hair much longer and more flowing, which gives the legs the appearance of being very short. This is the prevailing breed of the western isles of Scotland." This, of course, will answer for a description of our ordinary Skye terrier. Then of the third variety, which may be taken to be the ordinary or mongrel variety, the writer in the "Sportsman" says this "is much larger than the former two, being generally from 15 to 18in. in height, with the hair very hard and wiry, and much shorter than that of the others. It is from this breed that the best bull terriers have been produced."

Whoever wrote the above I do not know, but Thomson Gray, in his "Dogs of Scotland," makes a similar quotation, which he says is from "Brown's Field Book," also published in 1833. However, I take the description to be interesting.

What to me appears to be the strangest part of all, is that even the Highland sportsmen of that time, and a little later, called their native terrier the Skye terrier. St. John in his "Highland Sports" (1846) alluded to some of his terriers as Skyes, when they were undoubtedly our "die-hards." The long silky-coated dogs of the western isles would have been no use to a sportsman such as he, and although game enough in their way, they, the Skyes, did not possess the activity nor the power to tackle the wild cat, the marten, and other vermin found in the wilds of

Sutherlandshire, where Charles St. John lived. Moreover, he also calls them " Highland terriers."

He says, " Why do Highland terriers so often run on three legs—particularly when bent on mischief? Is it to keep one in reserve in case of emergencies? I never had a Highland terrier who did not hop along constantly on three legs, keeping one of them up as if to rest it.

" The Skye terrier has a great deal of quiet intelligence, learning to watch his master's looks and understand his meaning in a wonderful manner. . . . This dog shows great impetuosity in attacking vermin of all kinds, though often his courage is accompanied by a kind of shyness and reserve; but when once roused by being bit or scratched in its attacks on vermin, the Skye terrier fights to the last, and shows a great deal of cunning and generalship as well as courage. Unless well entered when young they are apt to be noisy, and yelp and bark more than fight. The terriers I have had of this kind show some curious habits, unlike most other dogs. I have observed that when young they frequently make a kind of seat under a bush or hedge, where they will sit for hours together crouched like a wild animal. Unlike other dogs, too, they will eat (though not driven by hunger) almost anything that is given them, such as raw eggs, the bones and meat of wild ducks or wood pigeons and other birds that every other kind of dog, however hungry, rejects with disgust. In fact, in many respects their habits resemble those of wild animals. They always are excellent swimmers, taking the water quietly and fearlessly when very young."

My favourite author then proceeds to write of their use in taking his master quickly up to a wounded deer, but, irrespective of the latter, no one can say that St. John's description does not altogether tally with that of the Scotch terrier. It is nearly twenty years since the late Captain Mackie gave me a small, semi-prick eared dog he had got from the north of Scotland, from which the above description might have been taken. It ran at times on three legs, was slow to be the aggressor, but was a terrible punisher for a fourteen pound dog when he did start ; and he, too, was at times shy and reserved, and would eat grouse and pigeon as freely as he would any butchers' meat.

Long before I owned this dog a friend of mine had a similar one sent out of Caithness-shire, which was called a " Skye terrier," but again he turned out to be just a Scottish little fellow, short on the legs, hard in coat, and as game as possible. Both these were brown brindles in colour, which I fancy were at that time more plentiful than the black brindles or almost black dogs, oftener seen on the show bench to-day.

It was about the year 1874 that a newspaper controversy brought the Scottish terrier prominently before the public, and the Crystal Palace shows and the one at Brighton the following year, viz., in 1876, provided classes for them, which, however, failed to fill. Then there came a lull, a club was formed, and in 1879 Mr. J. B. Morrison, of Greenock, was invited to the Alexandra Palace show to judge the Scotch terriers in a class which had been provided for them. A few months later divisions were given them at the Dundee show, when the winner, though a pure " Scottie," was called a Skye terrier, and came from that island. Birmingham provided a class in 1881, and with an incompetent judge the prizes were withheld, though such men as the late Captain Mackie, Mr. Ludlow, and Mr. J. A. Adamson were exhibitors. The Curzon Hall show appears to have been rather unfortunate in this sort of thing, for previously the leading prize in wire-haired fox terriers was withheld when there was as good a specimen of the variety as we ever saw on the bench or in the ring at any time. However, another year things went better with the Scottish terriers, as in 1883 Messrs. Ludlow and Blomfield, of Norwich, to whom much of the credit for the popularisation of the breed is due, again made entries and won chief honours with their little dogs Rambler and Bitters. Two years later Captain Mackie was the most successful competitor, securing the leading prizes with his historical Dundee and his lovely little bitch Glengogo, and so we are brought right down to the present time.

Much has been written of the various strains of the Scottish terrier, but such are of little account, as, although they were kept by many of the Highland sportsmen on their estates, and used for hunting purposes and for killing vermin, all had sprung from a common origin. They had not sufficiently distinguishing features from each other to merit a separation, though every laird said his own breed was the best and the only one to be found in its original purity. However, be this as it may, there is no doubt in my mind that this terrier had inhabited Scotland long before modern writers told us what they knew about dogs, and that all the stories about the Skye terriers being in reality a half-bred poodle or Maltese, made so by one of the breed washed up from a shipwrecked vessel on the coast of Skye, is all nonsense—a traveller's tale and no more. The so-called Aberdeen terrier is the Scottish terrier pure and simple, and the Poltalloch terrier, mentioned in " Dogs of Scotland," is a yellowish white variety kept by the Malcolms at Poltalloch, in Argyllshire, where the strain is carefully preserved. These terriers only differ in colour from the ordinary Scottish terrier. A white puppy occasionally appears in a litter of the latter as it does sometimes in deer-hounds Of course, if these white puppies were reared and bred from, a strain of that colour would eventually be perpetuated, and probably this has been the case in the first instance at Poltalloch. Some years ago Mr. Thomson Gray procured a white bitch of pure pedigree for Captain Keene, a well-known member of the Kennel Club. I have a portrait of her by me now, and she is certainly a Scottish terrier in every particular, and a great favourite with her owner, who entered her in the " Stud Book" as White Heather. From her, Captain Keene has had three litters to ordinary coloured dogs of the breed, but not one of the puppies has yet taken after their dam, all of them, strangely enough, being either black or very dark brindle.

It is a somewhat remarkable fact that this white Scottish terrier is occasionally produced in the ordinary course from dark coloured parents ; the Scottish deerhound likewise, but not frequently, throws a similar puppy in the same way, and Mr. J. Pratt has been successful in breeding two or three Skye terriers pretty nearly pure white. In alluding to these off coloured specimens one must not forget that fawn or sandy Scottish terriers are by no means infrequent, and two or three years ago Mr. A. Maxwell, of Croft, near Darlington, won several prizes with a dog of this colour, and a very good specimen of his race too. We all know that the fawn colour in deerhounds and in Skye terriers, although not so prevalent as once was the case, is still by no means uncommon.

The allusion to the Poltalloch terrier in the " Dogs of Scotland " elicited the following communication from Col. Malcolm, R.E., to the author of the work in question: " The Poltalloch terriers still exist in the Poltalloch Kennels, and I hope that your recognition of them may make it more possible to keep them up. They are not invariably white, but run between creamy white and sandy. A good one at his best looks like a handsome deerhound, reduced in some marvellous way. They are gameness itself, and terrible poachers. They love above all things to get away with a young retriever, and ruin him for ever, teaching him everything he ought not to know. As for wisdom, make one your friend and he will know everything and do it. I have known one whose usual amusement was rat-killing, and who had never retrieved, go into a hole in tender ice and bring out a wild duck, because,

I suppose, he thought it a shame to waste it when his master had shot it. This chap had a great friend, a mastiff bitch, and he used to swim along water-rat infested streams, and she applying her nose to the landward hole would snort a rat out of his wits into the water, and into the terrier's jaws, who, silently swimming, was keeping pace with his friend. They are said in the kennels to have a trick of suddenly turning upon one of their number and putting it to death, and when they do this they leave but little mark of their work, as they eat their victim. They are kept for work—fox and otter hunting. They have consequently to be kept small, and without the power which seems to be of such value on the show bench. This could easily be got by feeding up, but then the dogs would be of no use in the fox cairns. As it is, they often push in between rocks they cannot escape from, and so the best get lost."

Of the original Scottish terriers some there were with semi-erect ears, others with prick ears, as so admirably produced in Mr. Wardle's picture at the commencement of this chapter. The prick ears are acknowledged now as the more fashionable, though I fancy years ago the semi-prick ear was the more common. I have seen some excellent little dogs with semi-erect ears, as good as those with erect ears, but the tyrant Fashion at present holds only the latter the correct article, and by his opinion we have to abide. Classes have been provided for each of the varieties at some of the leading Scottish shows, but those for dogs with their ears " down " have never been well supported. However, the fact must not be overlooked that as puppies the ears are usually carried thrown back or forwards, some even not attaining the correct and erect position until six or eight months old. The hard, crisp coat, too, does not always appear until the puppy is casting its first set of teeth. And this hard coat is a *sine quâ non*, and no prize ought to be given to any Scottish terrier unless the coat is thoroughly hard and strong and crisp and close —it is the hard-haired Scottish terrier, a fact which some judges have sadly overlooked. Another defect too common and often over-looked is to be found in the bat-like ears with round tips, which some breeders consider to point to a cross with an impure strain. However, they are very unsightly, and ought to act as a very severe handicap on dogs possessing such aural appendages.

There is no denying the fact, even if anyone wished to do so, which I do not believe is possible, that during the last half dozen years the Scottish terrier has advanced very much in popularity. It might have done so even to a greater extent had there not been the Irish terrier and the fox terrier, who had preceded him in the field. So far there has not been much change in his make and shape, although every now and then a cry out has been made about big dogs winning. The gradation to cause this is extremely simple and easy, and I believe that the climatic, domestic, and other surroundings of the Scottish terrier in the south have more than a tendency to make him grow bigger than he really ought to do. Originally few or any of the best strains ran to more than 18lb. weight at most; the majority of terriers were 4lb. below that standard. Still, when a dog is brought into the ring that in show form is 20lb., and he is good in all respects, it is a difficult matter to discard him on account of size. Thus he wins. Perhaps some time later he meets a still bigger dog, one that may run to 22lb. or 24lb., and it would be very difficult to, as it were, disqualify the latter on account of size alone. And so we have bigger dogs than many people believe to be the correct size, winning prizes.

Dundee, perhaps, when owned by Capt. Mackie, and after, did as much winning as any Scottish terrier. I fancy he of late years when on the bench, having grown wide in front and thick, would weigh not less than 24lb., and other dogs equally big have repeatedly been put into the prize lists at our leading shows. Indeed, one well-known English admirer of the variety says the great difficulty he has in breeding these terriers is to keep them small enough. In the show ring the only way would be for the club to make a hard and fast rule as to weight, and put each dog in the scale before awarding it a prize or a card of honour.

Another matter to guard against is the production of an inordinately long body and crooked fore legs. Now, it is all very well for Scotsmen to say that their terrier should have crooked fore legs, but why should he have them? There is no reason in the world why such a pretty little dog ought to be malformed, and crooked fore legs are a malformation. Until recently no trouble had been taken to have them as straight as they might be, and so the crooked legs cropped up, as they always have done and always will do with long heavy bodies to support—bodies indeed quite out of proportion to the limbs.

A well-known scientist at the Natural History Museum, South Kensington, on being asked his opinion as to the crooked legs now found on many varieties of the dog, said " the outward curve of the fore limbs of the dachshund (and I suppose of the Scottish terrier, although I do not know them so well) is an inherited deformity unlike anything in nature."

Mr. H. J. Ludlow, one of our oldest admirers of the variety, is likewise of my opinion as to the deformity of the crooked legs, and, in allusion to the above, says this statement from South Kensington is more of an argument in favour of straight fore legs in a Scottish terrier than all the asseverations that have been made by breeders of dogs crooked fronted, that a straight front means ruination. "I take it that if Nature thought bent fore legs were a necessary formation for animals that depend upon burrowing for their safety, nay, for their very existence, she would have produced the requisite curve in at least some of them. I am satisfied to have Nature for my guide in breeding, and so long as I produce terriers that have to follow and do to death these straight-legged diggers, I shall be content with the spades that I find she has supplied her creatures with rather than run after the 'inherited deformities' that some prejudiced persons go rabid over. Looking at the question from a show point of view, there can be no doubt that a terrier with straight fore legs is a far more taking animal than one with crooked limbs, and, if for that reason alone, Scottish terriers are, sooner or later, bound to be bred with fronts as straight as those of the animals they are taught to look upon as their hereditary foes."

We do not want the Scottish terrier as unwieldy as the Dandie Dinmont or as the dachshund. A more active animal than either is required—one that can climb over rocks both above and below ground, and follow hounds in his kind of fashion. We want him an active, symmetrical little dog, on short legs, with a deep chest, not too long in body—in fact, just such an animal as is produced on another page. Mr. Wardle has drawn me two Scottish terriers which, to my mind, in make, shape, character, length of head, &c., are perfection.

There has of late been a tendency to give prizes to dogs with unusually long and narrow heads. Now this is again wrong, for with undue length of head or face, the character of the dog is lost quite as much, even more than it would be were the head short and round and of the bull terrier type. Craze for long heads has done harm to the modern fox terrier, and I think no one will require attention drawn to the injury the collie has sustained by the introduction of long heads, which are quite foreign to the breed.

That I do not not stand quite alone in my opinion as to the size and weight of the Scottish terrier will be inferred from the following description, which Mr.

Thomson Gray gives in " Dogs of Scotland ":
" The greatest difficulty is to get straight legs and
ears tight up. My idea of a first-class specimen is
a very game, hardy-looking terrier, stoutly built, with
great bone and substance ; deep in chest and back
rib, straight back, powerful quarters, on short
muscular legs, and exhibiting in a marked degree a
great combination of strength and activity. In
several terriers shown the body is too long. This I
consider a grave fault, and by no means to be
encouraged. . . . Terriers built on such lines
are very active in their movements, and for going a
distance or taking a standing leap I do not believe
there is any short-legged breed of terrier can equal
them.

" The coat should be $1\frac{1}{2}$in. long, thick, dense,
lying close, and very hard, with plenty of soft undercoat ; tail straight, carried well up, well covered
with hair, but not bushy. The ears should be as
small and as sharp pointed as possible, well carried
forward, and giving the dog a " varmint " appearance. The skull should not be too narrow, being in
proportion to the terribly powerful jaw, but must be
narrow between the ears, these being carried well
up. If carried sluggishly they spoil the appearance
of the dog's head. The eyes should be small and
deep-set, muzzle long and tapering, and, as already

stated, very powerful; teeth, extra large for size of dog, and level.

"In colour I prefer a dark grey brindle, or warm red brindle. Lately very dark colours have been preferred, but, I think, this is a mistake, as they are not so readily seen in the dark, and with advantage a little lighter shade might be introduced. Still I would certainly prefer a very dark colour dog to one too light in hue. 15lb. or 16lb. bitches and 17lb. to 18lb. dogs are the weights I like best."

Mr. Thomson Gray further says, in a letter recently written: " While I am in favour of having the legs as straight as possible, I would not sacrifice bone and muscle to get this point, or make it a *sine quâ non* in judging, as most, if not all, of the best terriers of this breed are a little bent, and any really straight-legged specimens I have seen have been deficient in bone, inclined to be leggy, and shelly in build. Now it must be kept in mind that the Scottish terrier is first of all a compact, firmly-built terrier, showing extraordinary strength for his size, and to lose these attributes is to lose the strongest points in the breed. Straight legs may be made a fad as much as any other point, and fanciers are apt to run on one point to the detriment of the rest, thus spoiling the even balance of the whole dog. Keeping what I have said in view, I see nothing to prevent these dogs being bred with straight legs, at least so straight as not to be an eyesore to look at."

The Scottish terrier in character and disposition is charming, as a companion most sensible and pleasant. He has no unpleasant smell from his coat, nor does he carry so much dirt into the house from the streets of the town and from the country lanes as a Dandie Dinmont terrier. Another advantage he possesses is that he is not so quarrelsome with other dogs as many terriers are. He will fight, and punish freely, too, when he is attacked and really has to defend himself, but the few that I have owned were slow to set about it. But when they did! I never saw such little dogs with such big teeth, and which could make such big holes in the legs and ears of a bigger opponent. They will go to water well and to ground likewise, and for hunting rough gorse coverts for rabbits are as useful as any other dark-coloured terriers, but personally I prefer a white dog for the latter purpose, as not so likely to be taken for a rabbit and shot accordingly.

Some of the best Scottish terriers at the present time are owned by Mr. H. J. Ludlow, Gorleston, and Capt. Wetherall, Kettering, both of whom are most successful breeders and exhibitors, such dogs as the former's Brenda and Kildee, and the latter's

Tiree II., Buccleuch, and Queen of Scots being all excellent specimens. Mr. J. N. Reynard's Revival (a dog whose dam died during or just after whelping, and was brought up by hand) ; Mr. E. Thompson's Ivanhoe, Mr. D. Cellar's Dundyvan, Mr. R. Chapman's Heather Prince, Mr. Morton Campbell's Stracathro Vision, Mr. A. MacBrayne's Corrie Dhu and Cairn Dhu, are all quite in the first flight, and equal to anything in the same line that has preceded them. Then Mr. J. D. McColl, Glasgow; Mr. G. H. Stephens, Aberdeen; Mr. D. J. Thomson Gray, Dundee ; Mr. John A. Adamson, Aberdeen (one of our very oldest exhibitors and admirers of the breed, and whose Ashley Charlie was only beaten on two occasions), Mr. J. F. Alexander, Kerriemuir (who bred Whinstone, The Macintosh, and Argyle in one litter) ; Mr. W. McLeod, Maryhill ; Mr. H. Blomfield ; are all names well-known in connection with this charming variety of terrier, which I hope fashion will never change in character or displace.

The Scottish Terrier Club, established in 1889, has for its secretary Mr. A. McBrayne, Irvine, and there is also a Scottish Terrier Club for England, the older establishment of the two, of which Mr. H. J. Ludlow is secretary. The description of the dog issued by the former is as follows :

" *Skull* (value 5).—Proportionately long, slightly domed, and covered with short, hard, hair, about ¾in. long or less. It should not be quite flat, as there should be a sort of stop, or drop, between the eyes.

" *Muzzle* (value 5).—Very powerful, and gradually tapering towards the nose, which should always be black and of a good size. The jaws should be perfectly level, and the teeth square, though the nose projects somewhat over the mouth, which gives the impression of the upper jaw being longer than the under one.

" *Eyes* (value 5).—Set wide apart, of a dark brown or hazel colour ; small, piercing, very bright, and rather sunken.

" *Ears* (value 10).—Very small, prick or half prick (the former is preferable), but never drop. They should also be sharp pointed, and the hair on them should not be long, but velvety, and they should not be cut. The ears should be free from any fringe at the top.

" *Neck* (value 5).—Short, thick, and muscular ; strongly set on sloping shoulders.

" *Chest* (value 5).—Broad in comparison to the size of the dog, and proportionately deep.

" *Body* (value 10). — Of moderate length, not so long as a Skye's, and rather flat-sided ; but well ribbed up, and exceeding strong in hind quarters.

" *Legs and Feet* (value 10).—Both fore and hind legs should be short, and very heavy in bone, the former being straight or slightly bent, and well set on under the body, as the Scottish terrier should not be out at elbows. The hocks should be bent, and the thighs very muscular ; and the feet strong, small, and thickly covered with short hair, the fore feet being larger than the hind ones, and well let down on the ground.

" *Tail* (value 2½).—Which is never cut, should be about 7 inches long, carried with a slight bend, and often gaily.

" *Coat* (value 15).—Should be rather short (about 2 inches), intensely hard and wiry in texture, and very dense all over the body.

" *Size* (value 10).—About 16lb. to 18lb. for a bitch, 18lb. to 20lb. for a dog.

" *Colours* (value 2½).—Steel or iron-grey, brindle or grizzled, black, sandy, and wheaten. White markings are objectionable, and can only be allowed on the chest, and that to a small extent.

" *General Appearance* (value 10). — The face should bear a very sharp, bright, and active expression, and the head should be carried up. The dog (owing to the shortness of his coat) should appear to be higher on the leg than he really is ; but, at the same time, he should look compact, and possessed of great muscle in his hindquarters.   In fact, a Scottish terrier though essentially a terrier cannot be too powerfully put together.   He should be from 9 inches to 12 inches in height.

FAULTS.

" *Muzzle.*—Either under or overhung.

" *Eyes.*—Large or light coloured.

" *Ears.*—Large, round at the points, or drop.   It is also a fault if they are too heavily covered with hair.

" *Coat.*—Any silkiness, wave, or tendency to curl, is a serious blemish, as is also an open coat.

" *Size.*—Specimens over 18lb. should not be encouraged."

SCALE OF POINTS.

	Value.		Value.
Skull	5	Legs and feet	10
Muzzle	5	Tail	$2\frac{1}{2}$
Eyes	5	Coat	15
Ears	10	Size	10
Neck	5	Colours	$2\frac{1}{2}$
Chest	5	General appearance	10
Body	15		
	50		50

Grand Total, 100.

I need scarcely say that the teeth must be large, powerful, and white, and being undershot even in the slightest degree should ensure disqualification. An overshot or pig-jawed mouth ought to be a severe handicap, and if very pronounced, likewise disqualification. An uneven mouth in any terrier I consider a terrible fault, one so serious that all puppies which have their teeth uneven in the slightest degree would, if in my possession, be destroyed. Usually one can tell as soon as the puppy is born how its " mouth " will be, but in some cases it is as well to keep the youngster until it has got its adult teeth before discarding him, as, if the unevenness is not great in the first set of teeth, it may altogether disappear with the second growth.

THE TERRIER (SCOTTISH).

ORIGIN.—Nothing definite of this breed can be traced, though it was for years known in Scotland as the Skye terrier.

USES.—Unearthing vermin, badgers, foxes, etc.

* SCALE OF POINTS, ETC.

	Value.		Value.
Skull	7½	Tail	2½
Muzzle	7½	Coat	15
Eyes	5	Size	10
Ears	5	Color	2½
Neck	5	General appearance .	10
Chest	5		
Body	15	Total . .	100
Legs and feet . . .	10		

37

GENERAL APPEARANCE.—The face should bear a very sharp, bright, and active expression, and head carried up. The dog should look compact and be possessed of great muscle in his hind quarters. A Scottish terrier *cannot be too powerfully* put together.

HEAD.—Skull long, slightly domed, covered with short, hard hair about ¾ inch long or less; skull not quite flat. Muzzle very powerful, tapering toward nose, which should be black and of good size; jaws level; teeth square, though the nose projects somewhat over the mouth. Eyes wide apart, dark brown or hazel, small and piercing. Ears very small, prick or half prick, sharp-pointed, the hair not long, and free from any fringe on top.

NECK.—Short, thick, muscular; strongly set on sloping shoulders.

CHEST.—Broad and proportionately deep.

BODY.—Moderate length, rather flat-sided, well ribbed up, and exceedingly strong in hind quarters.

LEGS AND FEET.—Legs short, and very heavy in bone, the front ones being straight or slightly bent, and well set on under body; hocks bent; thighs very muscular; feet strong, small, and thickly covered with short hair.

TAIL.—About 7 inches long, carried with a slight bend, and *never* cut.

COAT.—Rather short (about 2 inches), intensely hard, wiry, and very dense.

SIZE.—About 16 pounds for a dog; 14 pounds for a bitch.

COLORS.—Steel or iron gray, brindle, black, red, wheaten, yellow, or mustard color. *White markings are most objectionable.*

HEIGHT.—Nine to twelve inches.

FAULTS.

Large or light eyes; silky or curly coat.

Mr. J. L. Little's (Newcastle Kennels, Brookline, Mass.)
CHAMPION "MODEL"

THE SCOTTISH TERRIER

Origin.—Nothing is definitely known of this breed, though it was for years known in Scotland as the Skye terrier.

Uses.—Unearthing vermin, badgers, foxes, etc.

*STANDARD.

General Appearance.—The face should wear a very sharp, bright and active expression, and the head should be carried up. The dog, owing to the shortness of his coat, appears to be higher on the leg than he really is, but at the same time he should look compact, and possessed of great muscle in his hind-quarters. In fact, a Scottish terrier, though essentially a terrier, cannot be too powerfully put together, and should be about 9 in. to 12 in. in height.

Skull.—Proportionately long, slightly domed, and covered with short, hard hair, about three-quarters of an inch long, or less. It should not be quite flat, as there should be a sort of stop, or drop between the eyes.

Muzzle.—Very powerful, and gradually tapering toward the nose, which should always be black and of a good size. Jaws perfectly level and the teeth square, though the nose projects somewhat over the mouth, which gives the impression of the upper jaw being longer than the under one.

Eyes.—A dark brown or hazel color; set wide apart, small, piercing, very bright, and rather sunken.

Ears.—Very small, prick or half-prick (the former is preferable), but never drop. They should also be sharp-pointed, and the hair on them should not be long, but velvety, and they should not be cut. Ears free from any fringe at the top.

Neck.—Short, thick, and muscular; strongly set on sloping shoulders.

Chest.—Broad in comparison to the size of the dog, and proportionately deep.

Body.—Of moderate length, but not so long as a Skye's, and rather flat-sided; well ribbed up and exceedingly strong in hind-quarters.

Mrs. Jack Brazier's (Bay Shore, L. I.)
" BLAIR ATHOL "

Legs and Feet.—Both fore and hind-legs short and very heavy in bone, the former being straight and well set on under the body, as the Scotch terrier should not be out at elbows. Hocks bent and the thighs very muscular; and the feet strong, small and thickly covered with short hair, the fore-feet being larger than the hind ones and well let down on the ground.

Tail.—About 7 in. long, never docked, carried with a slight bend and often gaily.

Coat.—Rather short (about 2 in.), intensely hard and wiry in texture, and very dense all over the body.

Size.—About 16 lbs. to 18 lbs. for a bitch, 18 lbs. to 20 lbs. for a dog.

Colors.—Steel or iron-grey, brindled or grizzled, black, sandy and wheaten. White markings are objectionable and can only be allowed on the chest, and that to a small extent.

FAULTS.

Muzzle : Either under or overhung. Large or light-colored eyes. Ears that are large, round at the points or drop. It is also a fault if they are too heavily covered with hair. **Coat :** Any silkiness or wave or tendency to curl is a serious blemish, as is also an open coat. **Size :** Specimens over 18 lbs. should not be encouraged.

*SCALE OF POINTS.

Skull	5	Legs and feet	10
Muzzle	5	Tail	2½
Eyes	5	Coat	15
Ears	10	Size	10
Neck	5	Color	2½
Chest	5	General appearance	10
Body	15		
Total			100

COMMENTS.

The continued efforts of one or two of our prominent fanciers to popularize this breed are at last bearing fruit and it looks now as if the public is beginning to appreciate this, one of the most charming terriers known to the "fancy." The dog is being taken into the household as a companion, and a right good one he is, too, and instead of all the good ones

Mr. H. J. Ludlow's (White House, Bromsgrove, Worcestershire, Eng.)
CHAMPION "KILMARN"

41

being held by one or two exhibitors, they are rapidly being distributed all over the country, showing that his sterling qualities are being recognized. Though this breed has been variously known as the Skye terrier, Scotch terrier, the Scot's terrier, the Highland terrier, the Cairn terrier and the Die Hards, the public now know him only as the Scottish terrier. " Scotty " should be every inch a terrier, not too long in body nor too long on the legs. In addition to the faults as quoted from the standard there might be added that most fanciers consider that the faulty ears as spoken of should carry a *very heavy penalty* with them. Absence of stop, a skull much domed, weak before the eyes, or eyes set close together or devoid of snap and life, and uneven teeth, are very undesirable qualities. A Scottish terrier can as easily be too wide in front as he can be too narrow. The body must not be too long nor be sway-backed, nor should it be barrel shaped. Crooked fore-legs are no longer wanted in this breed and they must be straight in all that the word implies, strong and muscular, a light-boned, crooked-legged, out-at-the-elbows dog being considered an abomination. In regard to the coat perhaps the word "crisp" might be added as expressing just another additional description. At all times it should be very dense and "storm resisting," as the dog is a most excellent water dog and fears nothing. He is perhaps the least prone of any of the terriers to "scrap" with every dog he sees, but when "it is up to him" he pays all scores then and there with his powerful jaws. Again, perhaps no dog, as a rule, breeds truer to type than this one, which makes it especially comforting when one commences mating. One can thus form some reasonable conjecture as to what the product will be or rather what it ought to be.

A word of advice to the prospective buyer of a Scottish terrier. The Club's standard calls for "straight fore-legs" but it does not enumerate crooked ones among the "Faults." If one will only look about the shows for straight fore-legs in the Scottie he will be surprised to find how few there are that can with even the greatest charity be called "straight." If exhibitors are talked with in relation to this defect many will say "we don't require them straight." This is not true. They *are* required but they are very difficult to get, so in purchasing either a dog or a bitch for breeding purposes look well to the straightness of the fore-legs as the time is not very far distant when the crooked ones will be heavily penalized. There is no earthly reason why they should be crooked but there is *every* reason why they should be straight.

Mr. Fayette C. Ewing's (Nosegay Kennels, Webster Groves, Mo.)
"Baberton Lass"

From photo by Alfred Ellis & Wallery, Baker Street

MR. W. S. GLYNN

From photo by Kitchener & Salmon, New Bond Street

MR. W. S. GLYNN'S SCOTTISH TERRIER BRYNHIR BABY

Mrs. Hannay

THIS lady, known to many of my readers as one of our fanciers in the North, who is very often seen at shows in the Midlands and South, has always been a lover of animals in general and dogs in particular.

Of late years she has almost exclusively confined her attention to Scottish Terriers, with which she has been most successful at many leading shows and under the best judges of the variety.

I may mention Champions Gair, Villain, and Heworth Rascal, Lauriston Lass,

MRS. HANNAY'S SCOTTISH TERRIER CHAMPION
HEWORTH RASCAL

Heworth Merlin, Heworth Mite, Heworth Kate, Heworth David, Heworth Sandstone, and Heworth Diver as a few of the inmates of the Heworth kennels, but to set out all the honours taken would require more space than I am able to devote to them. I think, however, the praise I have elsewhere given to Scottish Terriers as all-round dogs and companions has been verified and confirmed by the enthusiasm they have evoked in this and other fanciers of the fair sex who have had a great deal to do with them, and I hope we may see many more high-class specimens emanating from the Heworth kennels, whose mistress takes much pleasure in her dogs,

45

MRS. HANNAY'S SCOTTISH TERRIER CHAMPION GAIR

and is a recognised figure amongst Doggy People.

The portraits of Mrs. Hannay and her Scottish Terriers Champions Gair and Heworth Rascal, particulariy good of each, are given with this slight sketch,' by their owner's courtesy.

C. H. LANE'S SCOTTISH TERRIER FRAOCHEN

From a drawing by R. H. Moore

MR. W. W. THOMSON'S SCOTTISH TERRIERS

CRON SOOTIE   CRON DIRK

From photo by Kitchener & Salmon, Bond Street, W.

MR. C. H. WOOD'S SCOTTISH TERRIER CHAMPION
BALMACRON THISTLE

Captain Tom Wetherall

Most of the many admirers of Scottish Terriers will know the subject of this sketch, who has long been a staunch supporter of that variety, and shown ability and judgment in the typical stuff he has brought out from his kennels, I think almost without exception of his own breeding.

When the Captain left his old regiment (the Inniskillen Dragoons), with which he served in the Crimea, he settled down in Northamptonshire, and has devoted himself chiefly to his favourite hobbies— horses and dogs.

When I mention the names of some of his dogs, many of my readers will remember what a

From photo by Speight, Kettering

CAPTAIN TOM WETHERALL

good stamp they were. Amongst the best known are Burris (who took second prize at the Crystal Palace in 1883, at the show held in January that year), Champion Tiree (a very high-class typical animal, nearly black in colour, very showy, and winner of many prizes whenever shown), Staffa (a charming bitch), Rawnoch, Tiree II., Kilbeth, Scotch Reel, Queen of Scots, Knight Royal, Gipsy O'Brae, Scottish Jewel, Queen of Night, Country Lassie, Gay Scot, Royal Irvine, Special Scotch, and others.

From photo by H. A. Marlee, Sunderland

CAPTAIN TOM WETHERALL'S SCOTTISH TERRIER
CHAMPION TIREE

To all who have the advantage of knowing him, I need not say that Captain Wetherall is one of those hearty, genial men whom it is always a pleasure to meet, and long may we have the benefit of his cheery presence at the gatherings of the Doggy People, with whom he is so universally popular and esteemed.

This slight sketch of the above-named popular fancier is accompanied by a lifelike portrait of him and a picture of Champion Tiree, one of the best Scottish Terriers he has owned.

LITTER OF DR. FLAXMAN'S WHITE SCOTTISH
TERRIER PUPPIES

DR. FLAXMAN'S WHITE SCOTTISH TERRIERS
PILLENWEEM REGINA   PILLENWEEM BILLY

THE SCOTTISH TERRIER

SCOTLAND is prolific in Terriers, and for the most part these are long-backed and short-legged dogs. Such are the Dandie Dinmont, the Skye, and the Aberdeen Terriers, the last now merged in the class recognised at our shows as the Scottish, or Scotch, Terrier; but the old hard and short-haired "Terry" of the West of Scotland was much nearer in shape to a modern Fox-terrier, though with a shorter and rounder head, the colour of his hard, wiry coat mostly sandy, the face free from long hair, although some show a beard, and the small ears carried in most instances semi-erect, in some pricked.

The descriptions given by Youatt, Richardson, and "Stonehenge" are in practical agreement, and apply to the kind of Terrier spoken of. There has, however, been of late years a rearrangement of classes of Terriers, and it is with those now recognised by the several clubs and show authorities that we have to deal.

The dogs now recognised as Scotch Terriers are closely allied to the Skye Terrier, and by a number of gentlemen of Skye and the South-west Highlands were at one time called Skye Terriers. It was suggested that, as they presented sufficiently distinctive characteristics, they might form a separate class at our shows, under the name of Highland Terriers. The idea, but not the name, was adopted; indeed, the name has given rise to some discussion. Cairn Terrier was suggested, but not generally adopted; they have also been called the "Die-hards."

"Whinstone" insisted on the breed being called the Scottish Terrier. Under the words "Scots" and "Scottish" Dr. Ogilvie refers those who consult this dictionary to "Scotch," which, he says, "is the established word." As long as we get Scotch collops from Scotch bullocks, and Scotch whiskey from Scotch barley, to aid the digestion of the collops, we may surely have Scotch Terriers; and, at all events, the Terrier under any name will bite as sore.

Mr. J. Gordon Murray, in the First Edition of "British Dogs," described three strains of these Terriers, according to the localities in which they were reared, and, as will be seen, differing only in minor points. Of these he says :—

"The Mogstad Skyes were of a dark greyish colour, with wiry hair from 3in. to 3½in. long, with body low but long, and measuring well in girth ; legs stout and short, and well provided with very strong claws ; the greater part prick-eared, and all of them excellent workers.

The Drynocks are another very splendid breed of the original pure Skyes, closely resembling the common Scotch seal in colour, short, wiry hair, with body of a medium size, a good deal like the Mogstads, and all of them first-rate workers.

The Camusennaries are another famous breed of the very real and pure Skye Terriers, and derive their name from a wild and mountainous tract of land in Skye, extending from Coirnisk on the west to the Spar Cave on the east. The breed was originally reared there by a Lieut. Macmillan, long passed away ; the whole of them short, wiry-haired, like the afore-named breeds ; colour almost always dark all over, middle part of hair in many instances grey, but again dark next the skin, no white on feet or chest ; a thin, medium-sized prick ear, and very pointed ; and in every third or fourth litter a reddish-yellow one."

Among Scottish fanciers Captain Mackie did a great deal towards improving the breed, though his first love was for a dog of a type not now recognised—namely, the long, low, bat-eared Skye form. He was a man of remarkable force and energy, and, as is often the case with such men, of a singularly frank and generous disposition. On the subject of this Terrier he was an enthusiast, and undertook voyages among the Hebrides, and long and arduous journeys through the Western Highlands, collecting information, and purchasing the best specimens of the breed procurable, from the oldest known strains. The story of at least one of these journeys of discovery is excellently told in the " Dogs of Scotland," to which we refer readers for details. The result was that Captain Mackie soon got together a kennel of these Highland Terriers of acknowledged superiority.

As companion dogs of the Terrier group, the Scottish Terriers possess qualities that recommend them to many. They are hardy and plucky, will stand any weather, and are good for any amount of sport. Disposed to be impetuous and self-willed, they often require more than ordinary care in training ; but that is well repaid, for the material is good to work upon. Another advantage to many people is that—the coat being of a length and quality that does not long hold wet and dirt—these dogs may be allowed a place on the hearth-rug or the door-mat ; and those who want a dog, of whatever breed, to be really obedient, lovable, and well-behaved, cannot have the animal too much with them.

With regard to the popularity of the Scottish Terrier (Fig. 97) in this country, no better proof can be adduced than that afforded by the entries at shows of the present day, or by the number of registrations that are recorded at the Kennel Club. One has but to carry one's mind back twenty years to fully recognise the headway the compact little Terrier has made in the Fancy. Though in this respect, of course, not to be compared with the Fox-terrier and one or two other breeds that might be instanced, yet he has made a bold bid for the favour of the dog-fancying public, and the measure of success attained could hardly have been anticipated by

FIG. 97.—MRS. HANNAY'S SCOTTISH TERRIER CHAMPION VILLAIN.

even the dog's warmest admirers. As indicating the possibilities there are in breeding the Scottish Terrier, it is worthy of record that at least £250 has been paid for a first-class specimen.

To what, then, it may be asked, is this popularity due? Mainly, it may be said, to the exertions of a few ardent souls, foremost among whom were Mr. J. A. Adamson and Mr. H. J. Ludlow, both of whom were breeding, showing, and winning prizes a quarter of a century ago, and working with a will to make known, by every legitimate means, the game and hardy Terrier whose cause they had espoused. Later on we find Mr. Ludlow, in conjunction with Messrs. Blomfield, Hammond, and Spelman, rendering still further service to the breed by bestirring themselves to establish a Club, which was accomplished in 1887, and now lives and flourishes

55

exceedingly. It was about this time that Scotchmen woke up to the fact that there was money in the breed, and that, moreover, they were passionately fond of their native Terrier. Whether this is so or not matters but little ; for henceforth the admirers of the Scottish Terrier steadily increased, until it now boasts a strong phalanx of supporters on both sides of the Border, while even across St. George's its merits have duly been recognised.

Even at this lapse of time Mr. Ludlow as a breeder and an exhibitor stands pre-eminent. To him belongs the credit of not only having bred a host of champions, but also more winners than any half a dozen living fanciers—a record that will not be readily effaced.

To refer to all the owners entitled to be placed on the scroll of fame during the past twenty years would serve no good purpose. All that is called for is the enumeration of a few of the more noteworthy during that period, which is perhaps the most important in the history of the breed, as it has witnessed the gradual rise of the dog into favour, to the detriment, undoubtedly, of its near relatives the Skye Terrier and the Dandie Dinmont Terrier, both of which it has easily outdistanced in the race.

First and foremost there have been Mr. H. J. Ludlow, Mr. J. D. McColl, Mr. J. F. Alexander, Mr. R. H. Blain, Mr. W. W. Spelman, Mr. J. Nuttall, Mr. C. H. Wood, Mr. C. B. Allen, Mr. G. H. Stephens, Mr. W. McLeod, Captain Wetherall, Mr. Robt. Chapman, Messrs. Astley and Aston, Mr. P. Taylor, Mr. A. Kinnear, Mr. J. N. Reynard, Mr. A. MacBrayne, Mr. D. J. Thomson Gray, Mr. A. M'Kerrow, and Mr. H. Panmure Gordon. Even of this restricted list many, alas ! are not now with us.

Of the names just mentioned there is none that was more enthusiastic over the Scottish Terrier than the late Mr. D. J. Thomson Gray, a thoroughly practical fancier, keen critic, fair-minded man, and a ready writer. Some seven or eight years ago he contributed to the columns of *The Bazaar* a splendid series of papers upon the " Terriers of Scotland," and neither before nor since has anything more genuinely interesting in connection with dogs or truer to life been published in that journal. Writing of the Scottish Terrier, he says :—

" Few there be that know anything about dogs that do not recognise the perky little chap called the Scottish Terrier. He is by no means an old resident south of the Tweed ; for it is only some twenty years since he was introduced to the southern dog-public. But from time immemorial the breed has existed in the Highlands and islands of Scotland, the daily companion of the fox-hunter, a solitary individual quite distinct and far removed from your English fox-hunter. The Highland fox-hunter lives in a small thatched sheiling, often remote from civilisation, his sole companions being a variety of Hound and a brace or two of Scottish Terriers. With an old gun his *tout ensemble* is complete. The Terriers oust the fox from the cairns (a collection of stones), and the old man polishes him off with his musket. If he misses or only wounds Reynard, the Hound is laid on, and finishes the job. But sometimes Reynard is able to baffle the old man with his Terriers, Hound, and gun, and escape scot free.

In temperament the Scottish Terrier somewhat resembles the English Fox-terrier. I say *English* Fox-terrier for, I may here explain that the Scottish Terrier in his native glen is called a Fox-terrier. Both breeds are of active habits, and are, as working dogs, used for the same purposes.

As behoves a resident in a cold and damp climate, 'Scottie' is clothed with a more rugged and more closely built coat, and his build and general appearance are more allied to the workman than the swell. All the same, Scottie is a gay fellow when he is properly dressed up—not faked—and he is ready at any time to fight for his place. One thing observable in these Terriers is that they are not quarrelsome among themselves. They are very easily kept under control, much more so than the Dandie, but they are not wanting in 'go.' For workmen these Terriers must be small, some of them being little over half the size of the ordinary show dog. Weedy? No; far from it. The wee dog has a big heart, and it is not size that gives pluck; moreover, the dog is not wanted to worry, but to bolt the fox or otter, as the case may be, by continual snapping at him and making him 'flit.' He must, however, have sufficient pluck to stick to his game until he bolts; otherwise he is useless. Unless Scottish Terriers are small they are of no use to oust foxes from the hill cairns, or otters from the rocks on the seashore or river-bank. Those who have followed the fox know how small a hole he will pass through, and unless the Terriers are small, they cannot reach him. As it is some of them get jammed in the rocks by dislodging stones in scraping to get at the fox, and never come out again.

The working Scottish Terrier is a good water-dog, and it is a pretty sight to see three or four lay hold of an otter in the water, although it is a very risky business. For hunting in broom and whin (furze) he is well adapted, as he makes things lively for bunny. He gives tongue when hunting, and is sometimes very noisy when game is in sight. Scottie likes to amuse himself by hunting up and killing rats; but he is at all times a companion and a 'friend in need' to the country gentleman or the rural dweller.

In the Highlands the principal colours are red and dark brindles. Sometimes fawns of different shades turn up; but white specimens are only to be found at Poltalloch, where they are bred and carefully preserved. A good many of the fox-hunter's dogs are coloured like their Deerhounds—a tawny brown—with often a white paw and sometimes a whole white leg. This no doubt arises from careless breeding.

Fanciers of recent years have tried to alter the original type of Terrier, by trying to engraft on a short, cobby body a long, senseless-looking head, to get which they had to breed dogs almost, if not quite, twice the size of the original, and to alter the formation of the head. That great Scotsman Thomas Carlyle said of Lord Ashley, ' Very straight between the eyes—a bad form of physiognomy.' Yes, bad, I would say, whether in man or in dog. This straight-face craze began in Black-and-tan Terriers, extended to Fox-terriers, is seen in Bedlington Terriers, is now contaminating the Collie, and is threatening our national Scottish Terrier. Coats are also getting softer and more woolly in texture, as they are inclined to do when the dog is kept in the house as a pet, and not exposed daily to the elements. There is also a tendency in some strains to grow a long coat, which the 'improver' shortens by removing the hair by a process known as 'trimming.' Such coats have always a soft, furry feel, reminding one of a cat's coat instead of a pig's, the bristles which resemble the true coat of the Scottish Terrier."

Mr. Thomson Gray, in the above, drew no fancy picture of the game little dog he loved so well, and in every word that he wrote, whether praise or blame, was prompted by one idea—the mainten-ance of the working type of dog rather than the setting up of a fashionable beauty. The trimming to which attention is directed prevails and has prevailed for many years to an extent unknown outside the fanciers' circle. Mr. Ludlow, however, in his review of the Scottish Terrier in the *Kennel Gazette* for February, 1900, was most severe on the practice of trimming, which he condemned in no measured terms, and pointed out the danger to the breed that is run thereby. As Mr. Ludlow very truly says, there is nothing to prevent the painstaking exhibitor making the best of his Terrier, and if it stops at removing the "frill" and taking out all the dead coat, no great harm is done. But does it stop there ? Personally, he believes that in very many cases it stops nowhere until every bit of long coat has been pulled out, the sides of the head have been trimmed down pretty well to the bare skin ; and, in fact, until the animal has been thoroughly transmogrified. He then proceeds to state that if it comes to a matter of skilful barbering, the novice will have no chance, and, as in the case of Bedlingtons, and to a less degree in Dandie Dinmont Terriers, the Scottish Terrier will be left in the hands of the few who have the ability and will take the trouble to catch the judge's eye, to the possible disadvantage of a

far better Terrier badly shown.   Since Mr. Ludlow's words appeared
in print there has been a marked improvement in the direction of
coats, and doubtless with the new regulations of the Kennel Club
in respect of trimming the practice will eventually cease.   That
it is unfair to novices goes without saying ; while that it is a most
stupid and unnatural practice calculated to injure rather than
improve the individual is also equally true.   The remedy for long
and woolly coats is a simple one, and lies in the hands of the
breeder, and this is the only " improvement " that should be
allowed by the powers that be.   There can be no denying that the
breeder has genuinely improved " Scottie " with respect to his front.
Time was when his fore legs were not considered typical unless they

FIG. 98.—DR. FLAXMAN'S WHITE SCOTTISH TERRIER PITTENWEEM KING
KONG.

were crooked.   He has changed all that, and nowadays a crooked-
fronted dog would not be tolerated in the show-ring.   Why, therefore, should one be whose coat is only of the requisite length when
it is made so artificially ?
    With Scottish Terriers, as with all other breeds, nature is
occasionally sportive, and we therefore come across, now and again,
colours that, according to our somewhat restricted views, may be
considered " foreign " to the breed.   It is now very well known
that white Scottish Terriers have been produced, and that these have
found more or less favour.   Indeed, Dr. Flaxman, of Pittenweem,
Fife, has for some considerable time now familiarised frequenters
of the larger exhibitions with these colour-sports.   One of these
dogs is illustrated at Fig. 98.   The colour is usually a creamy-white.
The late Captain Keene was one of the first to place these

white Scottish Terriers before the public, and a few years ago a puppy out of White Heather by a dog of his known as White Victor and bred by Mrs. Keene was shown by Lady Forbes, and was "in the money." White Heather was the product of dark parents, and so also were some of the best specimens of Dr. Flaxman. These whites are, of course, judged upon the lines of their darker relatives. One difficulty with the white productions was in the nose-colour. The early specimens were flesh-coloured as to nose; but this has apparently now been got over, as the noses of those white Scottish Terriers shown by Dr. Flaxman have jet-black noses.

These white Scottish Terriers are by novices frequently confused with the Roseneath Terrier, which is a grey or a fawn, sometimes with black points, and to which Mr. Thomson Gray alludes above though not by that name; it is a very different-looking type of dog from the Scottish Terrier. It is found in all its purity at Poltalloch, Lochgilpead, Argyll, where Colonel Malcolm is very proud of this strain of Terrier, and is nothing like the Scottish Terrier as known to the show-bench, but is a modern representative of the dog that Mr. Thomson Gray refers to as the old Skye, or West Highland, Terrier. They are small dogs suited for the work that they are called on to perform—to oust the foxes from the positions that Mr. Thomson Gray so well and faithfully describes. In appearance it more closely approximates to a Skye Terrier, though not to the dog that we are accustomed to see at shows, such a dog, alike on account of its size and its length of jacket, being quite unsuited for serious work. Mr. J. C. Macdona, who a few years ago attempted to revive the Roseneath Terrier by providing classes at Cruft's Show, has kept the breed; while the late Queen also possessed a brace, one of which came from the Duke of Argyll's kennel, and the other from Donald Ferguson, the Lochgilpead fox-hunter.

So many novices are called upon to make a selection of a puppy practically from the nest that a hint on what to avoid may be useful. First as to the head: there must from the first be indicated the slightly domed skull; while the colour of the eyes and their shape are all-important. A typical "Scottie" should have an almond-shaped, dark hazel eye, a light, round, prominent eye being very objectionable, and a puppy possessing such should be avoided. Straight fore legs should be combined with promise of plenty of bone; those light in bone or crooked in leg are objectionable. Ear-carriage cannot be determined with certainty until after teething; but ear-placement can. In a puppy over teething see that the mouth is a good one; for a typical healthy specimen should possess a beautiful set of white teeth, and any premature decay noticeable in the permanent teeth should not be lightly passed over. A bad mouth is a serious blemish, whether in a show specimen or only in a companion dog. A few white hairs on the chest in the puppy coat generally moult out; but not so a white patch in the adult. The writer is averse to the kind of fore face in the adult that gives one the idea of a square muzzle; it is a modern innovation and contrary to the description issued by the Clubs.

So far as specialist Clubs are concerned, the Scottish Terrier is well provided, there being no less than four—the Scottish Terrier Club (England), founded in 1887; the Scottish Terrier Club (Scotland), founded a year later; the Northern Scottish Terrier Club, and the London Scottish Terrier Club, both founded in 1902.

Below is given the description of the Scottish Terrier as drawn up by the Scottish Terrier Club (England):—

Skull.— Proportionately long, slightly domed, and covered with short, hard hair, about ⅜in. long, or less. It should not be quite flat, as there should be a sort of stop, or drop, between the eyes.

Muzzle.—Very powerful, and gradually tapering towards the nose. which should always be black, and of a good size. The jaw should be perfectly level, and the teeth square, though the nose projects somewhat over the mouth, which gives the impression of the upper jaw being longer than the lower one.

Eyes.—A dark brown or hazel colour; small, piercing, very bright, and rather sunken.

Ears.—Very small, prick or half-prick (the former is preferable), but never drop. They should also be sharp-pointed, and the hair on them should not be long, but velvety, and they should not be cut. The ears should be free from any fringe at the top.

Neck.—Short, thick, and muscular; strongly set on sloping shoulders.

Chest.—Broad in comparison to the size of the dog, and proportionately deep.

Body.—Of moderate length, but not so long as a Skye's, and rather flat-sided; well ribbed up, and exceedingly strong in hindquarters.

Legs and Feet.—Both fore and hind legs should be short, and very heavy in bone, the former being straight, and well set on under the body, as the Scotch Terrier should not be "out at elbows." The hocks should be bent, and the thighs very muscular; and the feet strong, small, and thickly covered with short hair, the fore feet being larger than the hind ones.

The Tail which is never cut, should be about 7in. long, carried with a slight bend, and often gaily.

The Coat should be rather short (about 2in.), intensely hard and wiry in texture, and very dense all over the body.

Size.—From 15lb. to 20lb.; the best weight being as near as possible about 18lb. for dogs and 16lb. for bitches, when in condition for work.

Colours.—Steel or iron-grey, black-brindle, grey-brindle, black, sandy, and wheaten. White markings are objectionable, and can only be allowed on the chest and to a small exent.

General Appearance.—The face should wear a very sharp, bright, and active expression, and the head should be carried up. The dog (owing to the shortness of his coat) should appear to be higher on the leg than he really is; but, at the same time, he should look compact, and possessed of great muscle in his hindquarters. In fact, a Scotch Terrier, though essentially a Terrier, cannot be too powerfully put together, and should be from 9in. to 12in. in height.

SPECIAL FAULTS

Muzzle.— Either under- or over-hung.

Eyes.—Large or light-coloured.

Ears.—Large, round at the points, or drop. It is also a fault if they are too heavily covered with hair.

Legs.—Bent, or slightly bent at elbows.

Coat.—Any silkiness, wave, or tendency to curl is a serious blemish, as is also an open coat.

Size.—Specimens over 20lb. should not be encouraged.

SCALE OF POINTS

Skull	7½
Muzzle	7½
Eyes	5
Ears	5
Neck	5
Chest	5
Body	15
Legs and Feet	10
Tail	2½
Coat	15
Size	10
Colour	2½
General Appearance	10
Total	100

The Scottish Terrier

Sometimes spoken of as the " Die-hard," a name said to have been given to them by George, Earl of Dumbarton, owing to the pluck of a pack owned by him.

The title is certainly not a misnomer, these little Terriers of Highland descent still having the gameness of their ancestors, though many of them at the present time are only used as ladies' companions.

The terms "Aberdeen" and "Scottish" Terrier are—or should be—synonymous, though an inferior specimen of a "Scottie" has, and is, frequently sold to the unwary as an "Aberdeen." Another name is that of "Cairn" Terrier, which speaks

SCOTTISH TERRIER DOG CHAMPION HYNDMAN THISTLE.

A Trio of Scottish Terriers (Property of Mr M'Candlish).

for itself, these dogs having been expressly bred for hunting in the cairns, or spaces amongst heaps of rocks, etc.

Owing to their small size, they are admirably adapted for such purposes. Some will retrieve and take well to water; are good companions, and active house dogs. They are very hardy, consequently puppies are not difficult to rear, and fair specimens of the last-named can be had at two and three guineas apiece.

The following are the chief points of the Scottish Terrier.

Coat.—In point judging, 20 per cent. of the marks are allotted to the coat—so many are faulty in this respect. Outer coat must be very thick, short, and of a hard or wiry texture, and absolutely free from any sign of curl, or waviness.

Hair, 2 or 3 inches in length. Under coat, very dense.

The so-called "open" coat is a fault. The term is sufficiently explanatory.

Weight.—From 14 to 20 lbs. for dogs and a few pounds less for bitches.

Colour.—Not of great importance, but white markings are objectionable; less important on the breast, but better without any white hairs.

White specimens are rare.

Brindle, black, red, mustard, and iron-grey, are the

usual colours, the black and brindle shades being preferred.

Body.—Important (value 10). This should be short, so as to give the dog a sturdy, compact appearance.

Some Scotties are too long in the body.

Neck.—To be short and thick, ending in good, strong, sloping shoulders.

Chest.—Deep, well-rounded on to the shoulders, and plump.

Limbs and Feet.—Legs, short, big-boned, well-muscled, straight, though generally turned out at ankles, ending in large fore feet, and smaller well-padded hind ones. The same hard hairs should clothe the limbs. If soft, it is a fault.

Ears.—Erect, or semi (half) erect. Must never " droop " at tips. Should be covered with short hair.

Particular attention is paid, by judges to the carriage of the ears of the Scottie.

Eyes.—To be either dark brown or hazel, giving a lively expression to the face.

Head.—Rather long, and wide above the eyes. Most of the length is gained from eyes to nose.

Hair to be hard and short (not soft).

Muzzle.—Long, tapering, and very strong.

Sound teeth—exceptionally large—and tight lips are a *sine qua non.*

GROUP OF SCOTTISH TERRIERS (Property of Mr M'CANDLISH).

Height.—9 to 12 inches,

Clubs.—1. The English Scottish Terrier Society ; 2. Scotch Scottish Terrier Society.

"SCOTCH TERRIER"   "A WHITE TERRIER" "A SCOTCH TERRIER"

These two illustrations are from Sir William Jardine's " Natural History," 1840, the dog volumes IX. and X. being contributed by Lieut.-Col. Chas. Hamilton Smith

"THE SKYE TERRIER"

From a painting by A. Cooper, R. A., probably 1830; may have been earlier. Cooper lived 1787-1868

W. B. SMITH'S " SCOTCH TERRIERS"

CH. THE LAIRD

Property of the Craigdarroch Kennels, and doubtless the best Scottish terrier shown in this country

70

THE SCOTTISH TERRIER

THOUGH undoubtedly a very old breed, the Scottish terrier is quite modern so far as knowledge of the variety outside of restricted sections of northern Scotland is concerned. Before taking up the history of the Scottish terrier we must first ask our readers to thoroughly understand that not a word was ever written regarding this breed till about 1880. One can find no end of information about the Scotch terrier, but that was a different dog altogether. Dalziel in "British Dogs," 1880, expressed regret that such a useful dog as the Scotch terrier had not been taken up and made something of, and he described it as a rough-haired sandy dog, though they came darker. Dalziel was a Dumfrieshire man, if we are not mistaken, and described the dog just as we remember it from our boyhood. He stood fairly well upon his legs and ran about fifteen pounds as a usual thing. He was rough-coated all over, body and head, a somewhat bristly coat that stood out and was dense as well. That was the dog that was everywhere known as the Scotch terrier. The brace of terriers drawn by Smith gives a good idea of the dog, and so does Spink's Bounce in Stonehenge's group illustration, shown in the introduction to the terrier family, Chapter XXVI., only that there is a little too much lay down about his coat. There is no doubt, however, that the term Scotch was decidedly an elastic one and Lieut. Colonel Hamilton Smith gives no less than three Scotch terriers, all differing, and not one the present-day Scottish terrier. One looks like a drop-eared Skye, another like the low, rough black and tan of England, while the head of Fury is more like the little rat killer that Dalziel wrote about and we also knew.

Landseer introduced small, short-haired terriers in some of his Highland paintings, a mongrelly lot, such as St. John mentions in his "Wild Sports of the Highlands," written about 1844, as accompanying the highland fox, or tod hunter "a miscellaneous *tail* of terriers of every degree." St. John does not discriminate in his use of Skye and Highland in his mentions of terriers. The illustration of his terrier with a few of his pets in our 1878 edition is probably modern and fanciful. Cooper's illustration of "The Skye Terrier" is undoubtedly the short-coated "Die Hard." The expression is somewhat that of his own black and tan rough terrier. This painting probably dates from about 1830, but may be earlier.

To go further back we have Captain Brown in his "Anecdotes" describing three varieties of Scotch terrier. One is the dog we have been writing about, another was the Skye terrier, though it is not named and is merely located as being the prevailing breed of the western islands of Scotland and with hair much longer than the first variety, and flowing. The third he describes ʳas fifteen to eighteen inches high, with a short, hard, wiry coat; and this he says was the dog from which the best bull terriers were bred. According to his own description it was only a larger specimen of his first variety. Youatt copied Brown's description, and it is evident that Brown did not know the Scottish terrier, nor did any person tell us anything about this variety till near 1880. About that time some of the English visitors to far north Scottish shows told on their return of a dog that looked like a short-haired Skye terrier and had the name of Aberdeen terrier. Some of these Aberdeen terriers were sent south to the Kennel Club summer show of 1879, although we do not remember seeing them at that show.

Under the name of Aberdeen terrier Dalziel devoted a chapter to the Scottish terrier, thus giving the first information in book form regarding the dog. At the same time and in the chapter on the Skye he gives a great deal of space to contributions regarding a short-haired terrier from the west coast, which Mr. J. Gordon Murray called the Highland terrier, and divided the breed into "mogstads," "drynocks" and "camusennaries." We might as well say here that it was this Highland terrier which Stonehenge repudiated *in toto* and called a very ugly brute, notwithstanding which he is quoted at times in support of the breed he scored as a nondescript.

Dalziel was quite right when he corrected Mr. Murray's claim for breeds under the outlandish names just quoted and said they were merely local varieties. They came from the same places that the Skye terriers were found, and Mr. Murray repudiated the Skyes altogether as mongrels of half poodle extraction, claiming that the ones he described were the "very real and pure Skye terrier." Mr. Murray contributed the illustration, or provided the dog for A. H. Moore to sketch, and we thus have the first

CH. NEWCASTLE MODEL
Property of Mr. J. L. Little, Brookline, Mass.

CH. HEWORTH MERLIN
Property of Craigdarroch Kennels

BETSY ROSS
An early Craigdarroch champion

CH. SILVERDALE QUEEN
Property of Craigdarroch Kennels

EMS CHEVALIER

CH. EMS COSMETIC

CH. LOYNE RUFFIAN
One of Dr. Ewing's first importations

GROUP OF EMS SCOTTIES
Property of Mr. W. L. McCandlish, Clifton, Bristol,
England

73

illustration of a Scottish terrier, labeled "Mr. J. Gordon Murray's Skye terrier Otter."

Then ensued a war fought with all the stubborn determination of the Scotchman when he is sure his cause is just. "This west country dog is only an Aberdeen terrier and must be known as such." "Not at all, the Aberdeen terrier is merely a stray from the western highlands and must be called Highland terrier." Thus they argued and wrote till someone suggested that as it was all Scotland anyway, why not call them Scottish terriers? This not being a victory for the opposition each side agreed, and thereby came the name of Scottish for the game little "Die hard."

There was also a discussion as to the ears being erect or tipping like a collie's, but that was settled in favour of the straight ear, although the old standard says they may be pricked or half pricked. After which all parties settled down to the business of breeding and improving the Scottish terrier and pushing it into a prominent position worthy of its national name. That they have succeeded in so doing the records attest, and the Scottish terrier is one of the most popular in England at the present time. In the early days of the fancy across the Atlantic the late Captain Mackie was very prominent in its support, and another who did much good work in the same direction was Mr. H. J. Ludlow, to whom is due the credit of breeding no less than twelve English champions.

The Scottish terrier's career in this country has not been a bed of roses, but rather on the order of the national "flower" of its own country. It was taken up with a vim by Mr. Brooks and Mr. Ames of Boston, and one or two others some years ago, but there was no getting the public to take to it. It did not attract, hence there was no popularity and we can recall the time when Mr. Brooks could not even give some of his young stock away. After that the ebb tide ran out so far that it looked as if it would never turn to flood again, but along came a Westerner with a reserve stock of enthusiasm, and back came the Scottie with a rush that carried it to a well earned high-water mark. A club was established and the breed put on a substantial foundation, thanks to the energy of Dr. C. Fayette Ewing of St. Louis.

To go back to the beginning of the Scottie in America means the recording of the importations of Mr. John H. Naylor of Chicago, the pioneer exhibitor of the breed, who was showing Tam Glen and Bonnie Belle in 1883. His next importation was Heather, and at New York in 1884 Heather beat Tam Glen in the class for rough-haired terriers. This brace did good service for Mr. Naylor, but of course they were not quite up to modern show form, though good little dogs and typical.

From a class for rough-haired terriers, the New York classification advanced to Scotch and hard-haired terriers, and in that class as late as 1886 Mr. Prescott Lawrence showed two Airedales, the only entries. In 1888 a class for Scotch failed to secure an entry. In 1890 three entries were made, "Scotch" Bailey showing the winner in Meadowthorpe Donald, with Mr. Naylor's latest importation, Rosie, in second place. So far the fancy had dragged along, but now the Toon and Symonds combination took up the importation of terriers and Kilstor was shown by them in 1891, taking first at New York and five other shows. For 1892 the same firm had Scotch Hot for first at New York, defeating Kilstor, next to whom came Glenelg, shown by Mr. T. H. Garlick, of Philadelphia, who still keeps in touch with the breed and frequently officiates in the distribution of awards, though he is more of a wire-haired terrier man now.

With 1892 came the boom in the breed, and the Wankie Kennels, which was the exhibiting name of the Messrs. Brooks and Ames, began a most successful career. In the kennel were such good dogs as Kilroy, Kilcree, Culbleau and others, and at New York in 1893 all three first prizes went to the Wankie Kennels, the classification being a mixed challenge class and two open classes. Toon and Symonds then got Tiree and Rhuduman and it was not long before the Wankie Kennels concluded to purchase the pair. Tiree was a grand little dog, and we are under the impression that he won a special for the best in the show at Philadelphia in 1893, though the catalogue has no mention of such a special.

The year 1895 at New York marked a high record for the breed, when no fewer than thirty-nine Scottish terriers were shown. Two American bred classes, the first for any breed, if we mistake not, since the old times of "native" setters. In these classes fourteen of the fifteen were duplicate entries and two puppies were also duplicates, raising the total entry to fifty-five. Of the thirty-nine dogs, sixteen were from the Brooks-Ames kennel and seven from the Newcastle Kennels of Mr. J. L. Little, and these exhibitors took fifteen of the nineteen prizes awarded, Mr. Little's modest share being a first and a third in open dogs, his first prize winner being Bellingham Bailiff, quite a successful dog in his day.

The natural result followed this one-sided distribution of the prize money and three years later we find the entry reduced to nine dogs and bitches. Mr. Brooks had retired by this time, but Mr. Ames took all three firsts that were awarded, that in the novice class being withheld, in which he however took second and third. He left only two second prizes to his opponents. This was Mr. Ames's last entry at New York. In 1899 Dr. Ewing made his first exhibit at New York, sending on entries of Loyne Ginger and Romany Ringlet, both English winners, although Loyne Ginger was then decidedly past his prime. The following year saw the importation of two very good terriers which found their way to the Newcastle Kennels; Newcastle Model and Newcastle Rosie, both of which won firsts at New York and did well elsewhere. There was not much life in the breed however, though those interested soon woke up or were aroused to the advisability of doing something. Dr. Ewing in the most energetic manner took hold of the formation of a club to look after the interests of the breed, and what can be done by concentrated effort was well shown by the entry at New York for 1901, when thirty-one dogs were entered, duplicates raising the entry to about fifty. Dr. Ewing won high honours with a puppy of his own breeding, Nosegay Sweet William, the prefix being his adopted kennel name. Another prominent winner on this occasion was Mrs. Brazier, who now shows as the Craigdarroch Kennels, and has ever since that year played a leading part as the prominent exhibitor of the breed.

Other exhibitors during the past few years have been Mrs. G. S. Thomas, the Brandywine Kennels, A. J. Maskrey, the Sandown Kennels of Mrs. E. S. Woodward, Mrs. George Hunter and Mrs. H. T. Foote, while there are quite a number of exhibitors who have but one or two dogs that they enter at many shows in the East. It is surprising to note how exceedingly popular the Scottie is with exhibitors who are prominent in other breeds, but take to the perky little customer as a house dog. Of course these exhibitors want good dogs, and these they also show and thus help to swell the entries. The result is that the Scottish terrier is vastly more popular than many imagine, and at New York this year the 1895 individual entry of thirty-nine was beaten by two, while the total entry with duplicates was forty dogs and twenty-one bitches. As illustrative of the success of the Craigdarroch Kennels it is only necessary to state that in the open dog class Mrs. Brazier had three dogs with the prefix of champion and two in the open bitch class had also the same title. Some of them are getting on in years and were then exhibited in all likelihood for the last time, but that grand dog The Laird is still not only able to win in his breed, but is a factor when it comes to a special for the best in the show.

Enough has been said to show that the Scottish terrier has made his way by his own merits to a warm corner in the hearts of his admirers, and that he is gradually growing in the estimation of the public and this not on account of any special attractiveness, but his smartness and cleverness as a companion and house dog. Guid gear goes in mickle bundles, is a Scotch proverb which applies most appropriately to this excellent little terrier. We ought to emphasise the word little by way of warning against any increase of size in this dog, for he is the smallest of the working terriers and must be kept so.

The illustrations we give of dogs here and abroad, together with the descriptive particulars in the standard, render it unnecessary to go into details as to the points of the Scottish terrier.

DESCRIPTIVE PARTICULARS

Skull.—Proportionately long, slightly domed, and covered with short hard hair about three-quarters of an inch long or less. It should not be quite flat, as there should be a sort of stop or drop between the eyes.

Muzzle.—Very powerful and gradually tapering toward the nose, which should always be black and of a good size. The jaws should be perfectly level and the teeth square, though the nose projects somewhat over the mouth, which gives the impression of the upper jaw being longer than the under one.

Eyes.—Set wide apart, of a dark hazel colour; small, piercing, very bright and rather sunken.

Ears.—Very small, prick or half prick, but never drop. They should also be sharp pointed; the hair on them should not be long, but velvety, and they should not be cut. The ears should be free from any fringe at the top.

Neck.—Short, thick and muscular; strongly set on sloping shoulders.

Chest.—Broad in comparison to the size of the dog, and proportionately deep.

Body.—Of moderate length, not so long as a Skye's, and rather flat sided, but well ribbed up and exceedingly strong in hindquarters.

Legs and feet.—Both fore and hind legs should be short and very heavy in bone, the former being straight or slightly bent and well set on

77

under the body, as the Scottish terrier should not be out at elbows. The hocks should be bent and the thighs very muscular; the feet strong and thickly covered with short hair, the fore feet being larger than the hind ones, and well let down on the ground.

The tail.—Which is never cut, should be about seven inches long, carried with a slight bend and often gaily.

The coat.—Should be rather short, about two inches, immensely hard and wiry in texture and very dense all over the body.

Size.—About sixteen to eighteen pounds for a bitch and eighteen to twenty pounds for a dog.

Colours.—Steel or iron grey, brindled or grizzled, black, sandy and wheaten. White markings are objectionable and can only be allowed on the chest, and that to a small extent.

General appearance.—The face should wear a very sharp, bright, active expression and the head should be carried up. The dog (owing to the shortness of his coat) should appear to be higher on the legs than he really is, but at the same me he should look compact and possessed of great muscle in the hindquarters. In fact, a Scottish terrier, though essentially a terrier, cannot be too powerfully put together. He should be from nine inches to twelve inches in height.

Faults.—Muzzle either under or over hung; eyes large or light coloured; ears large, round at the points, or drop; it is also a fault if they are too heavily covered with hair. Coat: Any silkiness, wave or tendencies to curl are a serious blemish, as is also an open coat. Size: Any specimens over twenty pounds should not be encouraged.

It should be the spirit and purpose of the judge in deciding the relative merits of two or more dogs to consider the approximation of nature to the standard rather than the effect of artificiality.

SCALE OF POINTS

Skull	5	Legs and feet	10
Muzzle	5	Tail	2½
Eyes	5	Coat	15
Ears	10	Size	10
Neck	5	Colour	2½
Chest	5	General appearance	10
Body	15		
Total			100

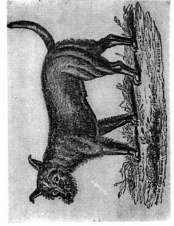

"THE SCOTCH TERRIER"

From Brown's "Anecdotes of Dogs," 1829. This book was published in Edinburgh, and Captain Brown was a Scotchman. This drawing has consequently a special authenticity

LADY CAROLINE MONTAGUE

By Sir Joshua Reynolds. Showing a dog, of decidedly more Scottish terrier character than was customary in paintings of his period (1723-1792)

STONEHENGE'S "UGLY BRUTE"

This is from Dalziel's "British Dogs," and is the illustration of J. Gordon Murray's Skye terrier Otter, which called forth Stonehenge's criticism of the new breed

THE SCOTTISH TERRIER.

BY WALTER S. GLYNN.

" *Losh !* *Bogie man, haud off your han' ;*
Nor thrash me black and blue.
Frae fools and foes I seek nae praise,
But frien's should aye be true.

" *Nae silky-haired admirer I*
O' Bradford Toys, Strathbogie ;
Sich thoughts, I'm sure cam' in your head,
While dribblin' o'er the cogie.

" *I ken the Terrier o' the North,*
I ken the towsy tyke—
Ye'll search frae Tweed to Sussex' shore,
But never find his like.

" *For pluck and pith and jaws and teeth,*
And hair like heather cowes,
Wi' body lang and low and strang,
At hame in cairns or knowes.

" *He'll face a foumart, draw a brock,*
Kill rats and whitteritts by the score,

He'll bang tod-lowrie frae his hole,
Or slay him at his door.

" *He'll range for days and ne'er be tired,*
O'er mountain, moor, and fell ;
Fair play, I'll back the brave wee chap
To fecht the de'il himsel'.

" *And yet beneath his rugged coat*
A heart beats warm and true.
He'll help to herd the sheep and kye,
And mind the lammies too.

" *Then see him at the ingle side,*
Wi' bairnies roond him laughin'.
Was ever dog sae pleased as he,
Sae fond o' fun and daffin' ?

" *But gie's your hand, Strathbogie man !*
Guid faith ! we maunna sever.
Then ' Here's to Scotia's best o' dogs,
Our towsy tyke for ever !' "

THE above lines are an excellent description of the Scottish Terrier. They appear over the name of Dr. Gordon Stables in *The Live Stock Journal* of January 31st, 1879. At about this time a somewhat fierce and certainly most amusing controversy was going on as to whether or not there was such a thing as a pure-

81

bred "Scottish Terrier." The pages of the above publication for the months of January, February, March, April, and May of that year are well worth reading by anyone interested in the subject of this chapter. He will find there several letters written by different enthusiasts, prominent among whom were "Strathbogie" (mentioned in the poem at the head of this chapter), "The Badger," Mr Russell Earp, Mr. (afterwards Sir) John Everett Millais, Dr. Gordon Stables, R.N., and Mr. Thomson Gray.

"Strathbogie" and "The Badger" were most anxious to make well-known in England the breed which they knew to be genuine. "The Badger" (Mr., now Sir, Paynton Pigott, M.V.O.) had undoubtedly in England a strong kennel of the right article, which he had gradually and quietly possessed himself of. "Strathbogie" (Captain Gordon Murray) appears to have been aware of this; but very few other people in England seem to have known of it, or, indeed, to have been aware that there was such a thing as a real Scottish Terrier in existence. They knew of the Dandie Dinmont, also of the Skye; and they knew also that the prizes in several classes for Scottish Terriers had been won by Yorkshire Toy Terriers, in glass cases, from Bradford. Some few there were who had a faint remembrance of seeing what were called Scottish or Highland Terriers when they were quite young, and had later, with unfailing want of success, tried to get hold of a specimen. Scotsmen themselves do not seem to have been very clear on the point, not only as to what a Scottish Terrier in reality was, but also as to where he existed and was to be obtained.

In 1877, about two years before, a tremendous controversy had waged for months in the columns of *The Live Stock Journal;* personalities were freely indulged in, and so inextricably mixed did the contributors become that the correspondence had perforce to be put an end to by the editor, the following note being attached to the last published letter : " We see no use in prolonging this discussion except each correspondent *describes* the dog he is talking about and holds to be the true type."

For some time this seems to have put an end to the correspondence, possibly because no one felt himself able to fulfil the editorial condition. However this may be, eventually, in January, 1879, we find the said " Strathbogie " again brings the matter up, writes to the said journal, and publishes therein his idea of what a Scottish Terrier should be. He deplores the fact that prizes go to mongrels with coats 10½ inches long, and says the Scottish Terrier should " be in colour either grey or iron grey; dark, with brown muzzle; legs brown or dark fawn, no white about them.

SIR PAYNTON PIGOTT'S GRANITE.
THE FIRST SCOTTISH TERRIER ENTERED AT A KENNEL CLUB SHOW.
Drawn by C. BURTON BARBER.

His head should be fairish long, strong muscular jaws ; ears small, dropping to the front ; body lengthy ; legs stout and well covered with muscle ; tail carriage, houndlike ; length of coat not over, if possible, 3 inches, which ought to be hard and dense ; weight from 12 lb. to 18 lb., not more, though I have known good specimens a trifle over this weight ; temper good, both with man and dog. Scotch Terriers are far from quarrelsome ; they are kind, quiet, and fond of each other. . . . I am astonished the K.C. does not give us a class for this famous breed."

It was this letter of "Strathbogie's" that brought forth as a rejoinder the verses which head this chapter, for in the said letter "Strathbogie" complains that in an article written some time previously by Dr. Gordon Stables on the breed, the doctor, a Scotsman, appeared to class Scottish Terriers with "the silly long-woolled Toys of Bradford," and he goes on to say, "Now I am not second to the funny doctor in my admiration (love, if you like) for 'flowing tresses,' still I prefer such to adorn the shapely head of a bonnie Highland lassie to seeing them covering the backs of Scotch Terriers"—a sentiment, no doubt, with which not one of the many male admirers of the Scottish Terrier of the present day will fall out. "Strath-

There can be no doubt that the present-day Scottish Terrier owes a great deal to "The Badger" and "Strathbogie." These two gentlemen, despite many setbacks, stuck to their point, and eventually were rewarded by the late Mr. S. E. Shirley, then President of the Kennel Club, who seems to have been very popular with Scotchmen—as, indeed, he was with everyone—granting their request and giving or getting

MR. A. G. COWLEY'S

CH. EMS CHEVALIER

BY CAMOWEN LADDIE——CARTER JEAN.

MR. J. DEANE WILLIS' CH. CARTER LADDIE

BY CAMOWEN LADDIE——CARTER JEAN.

bogie's" letter had also the effect of drawing from his lair "The Badger," who, writing shortly afterwards in the same periodical, says he quite agrees with "Strathbogie's" description of the breed, but adds that he fancies there are also some of a sandy colour, that their ears may be either drop or prick, and that he prefers them at 14 lb. to 16 lb. weight, long and low, with a hard wire coat and straight in the fore-legs, "though sometimes they will be found slightly bowed."

them two classes for their breed at the Kennel Club show of that year, held at the Alexandra Palace.

The Scottish Terrier as a show dog undoubtedly, therefore, dates from about 1877 to 1879. He seems almost at once to have attained popularity, and he has progressed gradually since then, ever in an upward direction, until he is—for he does in fact exist—to-day one of the most popular and extensively owned varieties of the dog. Sir Paynton Pigott had undoubtedly at that time a very fine kennel of the breed, for in *The Live Stock Journal* of May 30th, 1879, we find his kennel fully reviewed in a most enthusiastic manner by a correspondent who visited it in consequence of all the controversy that was going on at the time, as to whether or not there was such a dog at all, and who, therefore, wished to see and judge for himself as to this point. At the end of his report on the kennel the writer adds these words: "It was certainly one of the happiest days of my life to have the pleasure of looking over so many grand little dogs, but to find them in England quite staggered me. Four dogs and eight bitches are not a bad beginning, and with care and judicious selection in mating, I have little doubt but Mr. Pigott's kennel will be as renowned for Terriers as the late

Mr. Laverack's was for Setters. I know but few that take such a delight in the brave little 'die-hards' as Mr. Pigott, and he may well feel proud of the lot he has got together at great trouble and expense."

The fact that there was such a kennel already in existence proved, of course, a strong point in favour of the *bonâ fides* of the breed. The best dog in it was Granite, whose portrait and description was given in the *Journal* in connection with the said review; and the other animals of the kennel being of the same type, it was at once recognised that there was, in fact, such a breed, and the mouths of the doubters were stopped.

Granite was unquestionably a typical Scottish Terrier, even as we know them at the present day. He was certainly longer in the back than we care for nowadays, and his head also was shorter, and his jaw more snipy than is now seen, but his portrait clearly shows he was a genuine Scottish Terrier, and there is no doubt that he, with his kennel mates, Tartan, Crofter, Syringa, Cavack, and Posey, conferred benefit upon the breed.

To dive deeper into the antiquity of the Scottish Terrier is a thing which means that he who tries it must be prepared to meet all sorts of abuse, ridicule, and criticism. For an Englishman, or, indeed, nine-tenths of the population of Scotland to talk to the few Scotsmen who *do* know —or think they do—is heresy, deserving of nothing but the deepest contempt.

One man will tell you there never was any such thing as the present-day Scottish Terrier, that the mere fact of his having prick ears shows he is a mongrel; another, that he is merely an offshoot of the Skye or the Dandie; another, that the only Scottish Terrier is a white one; another, that he is merely a manufactured article from Aberdeen, and so on *ad infinitum.*

It is a most extraordinary fact that Scotland should have unto herself so many different varieties of the terrier. There is strong presumption that they one and all came originally from one variety, and it is quite possible, nay probable, that different crosses into other varieties have produced the assortment of to-day. The writer is strongly of opinion that there still exist in Scotland at the present time specimens of the breed which propagated the lot, which was what is called even now the Highland Terrier, a little long-backed, short-legged, snipy-faced, prick or drop-eared, mostly sandy and black-coloured terrier, game as a pebble, lively as a cricket, and all in all a most charming little companion; and further, that to produce our present-day Scottish Terrier—or shall we say, to improve the points of his progenitor?—the assistance of our old friend the black and tan wire-haired terrier of England was sought by a few astute people living probably not very far from Aberdeen. The writer feels the vials of the wrath of the Scotsman, the hiss of his breath, the hatred of his eye, and if it were not that they never do such a thing, he would add the curse of his lip ; but, for all of it, he is confident that he is right and whole-heartedly congratulates the gentlemen north of the Tweed on the animal they have produced.

The Skye, the Dandie, the White Scottish have no place in this chapter. Were it otherwise, nothing would be easier than to unfold the method by which they have been begotten. There can, with regard at any rate to the two first mentioned, in all likelihood be no mistaking the breed or breeds which have been employed for this purpose.

Scottish Terriers frequently go by the name of Aberdeen Terriers—an appellation, it is true, usually heard only from the lips of people who do not know much about them. Mr. W. L. McCandlish, one of the greatest living authorities on the breed, in an able treatise published some time back, tells us, in reference to this matter, that the terrier under notice went at different periods under the names of Highland, Cairn, Aberdeen, and Scotch ; that he is now known by the proud title of Scottish Terrier ; and that "the only surviving trace of the differing nomenclature is the title Aberdeen, which many people still regard as a different breed—a want of knowledge frequently turned to account by the unscrupulous dealer who is able to sell under the name of Aberdeen a dog too bad to dispose of as a Scottish Terrier." Mr. Harding Cox tells us that the name of Aberdeen as applied to Scottish Terriers dies hard, that it is still the name used amongst the non-technical cynophilists, and is stoutly supported by the

soi-disant wiseacre. All this is unquestionably true, as far as it goes ; but there can be no doubt that originally there must have been *some* reason for the name. In a letter to the writer, Sir Paynton Pigott says, "Some people call them and advertise them as the Aberdeen Terrier, which is altogether a mistake ; but the reason of it is that forty years ago a Dr. Van

MR. J. LEE'S MAULDEN RANNOCH
BY CH. HEWORTH RASCAL——BALMACRON DAISY.

Bust, who lived in Aberdeen, bred these terriers to a large extent and sold them, and those buying them called them, in consequence, ' Aberdeen Terriers,' whereas they were in reality merely a picked sort of Old Scotch or Highland Terrier." Sir Paynton himself, as appears from the columns of *The Live Stock Journal* (March 2nd, 1877), bought some of the strain of Van Bust, and therein gives a full description of the same.

"Strathbogie," however, would have none of the Aberdeen Terriers, and would not even admit there was such a dog. He endeavoured, previously in the same year, to put " The Badger " and Dr. Gordon Stables right on the point by telling them they were just about as correct as was a certain Lord Provost on an occasion when he was invited by a captain of a ship, who had returned from Jamaica, to dine with him on his ship and examine the wondrous cargo he had brought home. As the Provost and other dignitaries were sitting at dinner in the cabin, the former's pigtail was vigorously

MR W. L. McCANDLISH'S CH. EMS COSMETIC
BY EMS TONIC — CH. SEAFIELD BEAUTY.

pulled several times, and at last the Provost, being unable to stand it any longer, turned round and addressed the puller thus : "Come that gait again, laddie, an' I'll pit ye in the hert (prison) of auld Aberdeen." "What's the matter with you, Provost ? " said the captain. "Oh," said the Provost, "that laddie ye hae fasen wi' ye has been tug-tug-tuggin' at my tail, till the hair is near oot at the reets." " 'Laddie,' did ye say ? " replied the captain ; "why, that's a monkey," and monkey sure enough he was. "Monkey, do ye ca' it ? " answered the great man. "I thought it wis a Wast. Indian planter's son, come hame tae oor university for his education."

Sir Paynton Pigott's kennel of the breed assumed quite large proportions, and was most successful, several times winning all the prizes offered in the variety at different shows. He may well be called the Father of the breed in England, for when he gave up exhibiting, a great deal of his best blood got into the kennels of Mr. H. J. Ludlow, who, as everyone knows, has done such a tremendous amount

of good in popularising the breed and has also himself produced such a galaxy of specimens of the very best class. Mr. Ludlow's first terrier was a bitch called Splinter II., a terrier that has been called the Mother of all the breed and did a quite unfathomable amount of good to it. The name of Kildee is, in the breed, almost world-famous, and it is interesting to note that in every line does he go back to the said Splinter II. Rambler—called by the great authorities the first pillar of the stud book—was a son of a dog called Bon-Accord, and it is to this latter dog and Roger Rough, and also the aforesaid Tartan and Splinter II. that nearly all of the best present-day pedigrees go back. This being so, it is unnecessary to give, in this chapter, many more names of dogs who have in their generations of some years back assisted in bringing the breed to its present state of perfection. An exception, however, must be made in the case of two sons of Rambler, by name Dundee and Alister, names very familiar in Scottish Terrier pedigrees of the present day. Alister especially was quite an ex-

MR. JOHN LEE'S BITCH CH. MAULDEN RECORD
BY CAMOWEN LADDIE — POLLY.

traordinary stud dog. His progeny were legion, and some very good terriers of to-day own him as progenitor in nearly every

86

line. The best descendants of Alister were Kildee, Tiree, Whinstone, Prince Alexander, and Heather Prince. He was apparently too much inbred to, and though undoubtedly he produced or was responsible for several beautiful terriers, it is much to be doubted whether in a breed which is unquestionably nowadays suffering from the ill-effects of too much inbreeding, he was not, unwittingly, of course, one of the greatest sinners.

The Scottish Terrier Club was formed in the year 1882, it at first having joint secretaries, treasurers, and committees for England and Scotland, but afterwards, on the score of convenience, these sections were split up into different clubs, one for each country. Both exist at the present day, and both have worked well—though, occasionally, rather of the " fit and start " order—for the good of the breed. It is perhaps right to add that, although at times there has been a little jealousy between them, they are now working together most harmoniously and were never stronger or better managed than they are at the present time. Mr. H. J. Ludlow was for many years a popular Hon. Secretary of the English Club, a post which on his resignation was taken up by Mr. W. L. McCandlish, than whom no better gentleman for any such office ever lived. Mr. J. N. Reynard —a household name in Scottish Terriers— is the Hon. Secretary of the Scottish Club, which is equally well managed by him. Such is the popularity of the breed that several other clubs have been started, and one well worthy of mention, on account of the great success which has attended its efforts, is the South of England Scottish Terrier Club, a powerful and popular organisation which has done much further to impress the inhabitants in and around the Metropolis of the absolute necessity of owning a Scottish Terrier.

In the same year a joint committee drew up a standard of perfection for the breed, Messrs. J. B. Morison and Thomson Gray, two gentlemen who were looked upon as great authorities, having a good deal to do with it.

This standard is still the same as far as the English Club is concerned, though the Scottish Club has, it is believed, altered it in some not very important particulars.

STANDARD OF POINTS OF THE SCOTTISH TERRIER.

1. Skull.—Proportionately long, slightly domed and covered with short hard hair about ¾ inch long or less. It should not be quite flat, as there should be a sort of stop or drop between the eyes.

2. Muzzle.—Very powerful, and gradually tapering towards the nose, which should always be black and of a good size. The jaws should be perfectly level, and the teeth square, though the nose projects somewhat over the mouth, which gives the impression of the upper jaw being longer than the under one.

3. Eyes.—A dark-brown or hazel colour ; small, piercing, very bright and rather sunken.

4. Ears.—Very small, prick or half prick (the former is preferable), but never drop. They should also be sharp pointed, and the hair on them should not be long, but velvety, and they should not be cut. The ears should be free from any fringe at the top.

5. Neck.—Short, thick and muscular ; strongly set on sloping shoulders.

6. Chest.—Broad in comparison to the size of the dog, and proportionately deep.

7. Body.—Of moderate length, but not so long as a Skye's, and rather flat-sided ; well ribbed up, and exceedingly strong in hindquarters.

8. Legs and Feet.—Both fore- and hind-legs should be short and very heavy in bone, the former being straight and well set on under the body, as the Scottish Terrier should not be out at elbows. The hocks should be bent, and the thighs very muscular, and the feet strong, small and thickly covered with short hair, the fore feet being larger than the hind ones.

9. Tail.—Should be about 7 inches long, never docked, carried with a slight bend and often gaily.

10. Coat.—Should be rather short (about 2 inches), intensely hard and wiry in texture, and very dense all over the body.

11. Size.—From 15 lb. to 20 lb. ; the best weight being as near as possible 18 lb. for dogs, and 16 lb. for bitches when in condition for work.

12. Colour.—Steel or iron grey, black brindle, brown brindle, grey brindle, black, sandy and wheaten. White markings are objectionable, and can only be allowed on the chest and to a small extent.

13. General Appearance.—The face should wear a very sharp, bright and active expression, and the head should be carried up. The dog (owing to the shortness of his coat) should appear to be higher on the leg than he really is ; but at the same time he should look compact and possessed of great muscle in his hindquarters. In fact, a Scottish Terrier, though essentially a Terrier, cannot be too powerfully put together, and should be from about 9 inches to 12 inches in height.

Special Faults.

Muzzle.—Either under- or overhung.
Eyes.—Large or light-coloured.
Ears.—Large, round at the points or drop. It is also a fault if they are too heavily covered with hair.
Legs.—Bent, or slightly bent, and out at elbows.

Coat.—Any silkiness, wave or tendency to curl is a serious blemish, as is also an open coat.
Size.—Specimens of over 20 lb. should be discouraged.

Scale of Points.

Skull	7½
Muzzle	7½
Eyes	5
Ears	5
Neck	5
Chest	5
Body	15
Legs and feet . . .	10
Tail	2½
Coat	15
Size	10
Colour	2½
General appearance . .	10
Total . . .	100

The two points which strike the writer most in looking over the above standard and scale of points are, first, the small amount of points allotted to the tail, and, second, that a bent or *slightly bent* leg is to be looked upon as a special fault and therefore severely handicapped, equally, indeed, we must assume, with an undershot mouth. About 99 per cent. of the Scottish Terriers living to-day have bent or slightly bent fore-legs. Formed as he is, if he has plenty of rib and depth in body, it is extremely difficult to get, on a dog built so close to the ground, a quite straight leg. Breeders must, therefore, not take to heart too much this " special fault." A straight, properly placed leg on a Scottish Terrier is certainly a beautiful thing to look at, and one does occasionally see it, though what is usually to be seen with a straight leg is a badly placed shoulder and a dog not properly knit together, who walks wide in front and cannot help turning his elbows out. It is, of course, unnecessary to state that a good shoulder, with a slightly bent fore-leg, is far better for work than a bad shoulder with a leg attached to it altogether, as one might say, outside the body.

The tail of a Scottish Terrier is one of its great characteristics, and is, in the writer's humble opinion, meanly appreciated in the above scale of points. A long, thin tail is a most objectionable fault, and entirely spoils the character of a specimen of the breed. It is to be doubted whether, with the points as they are, and those allotted for general appearance being only ten, a gentleman judging strictly on points would find himself able sufficiently to handicap a specimen for this fault. In this connection it is worth noting that judges *do* consider scales of points when officiating ; they get into a way of going for those dogs possessed of particular points more highly appreciated in the scale than others.

There have, of recent years, been many very excellent specimens of the Scottish Terrier bred and exhibited. Pre-eminent among them stands Mrs. Hannay's Ch. Heworth Rascal, who was a most symmetrical terrier, and probably the nearest approach to perfection in the breed yet seen. Other very first-class terriers have been the same lady's Ch. Gair, Mr. Powlett's

Ch. Callum Dhu, Mr. McCandlish's Ems Cosmetic, Mr. Chapman's Heather Bob and Heather Charm, Mr. Kinnear's Seafield Rascal, Mr. Wood's Hyndman Chief, Messrs. Buckley and Mills's Clonmel Invader, and Mr. Deane Willis's Ch. Huntley Daisy and Ch. Carter Laddie.

As has already been stated, Mr. Ludlow had at one time a very strong—as well as extensive—kennel, and it is probably correct that he has bred more champions than anyone up to date. The breed is now so popular, and competition so keen, that it is much to be doubted whether it will fall to the lot of anyone else to be as successful in this line as he was. Mr. Chapman, of Glenboig, N.B., was another gentleman who had at one time a very powerful collection and was at the same time a most successful breeder. First, Sir Paynton Pigott dropped out, then Mr. Ludlow, then Mr. Chapman ; and the mantle of the lot seems to have fallen now on Mr. McCandlish, who seems to have, at any rate in bitches, the strongest kennel of to-day ; and nearly all his terriers are bred by himself. Mrs. Hannay has always had a strong kennel, and so have Mr. Reynard, Mr. Kinnear, Mr. Wood, and Mr. Cumming. Other successful breeders have been Mr. Cuthbert Allen, Mr. Peter Stewart, Mr. J. D. Brown, Mr. Irwin Scott, Mr. Cowley, the Rev. G. Fogo, the Misses Niven, Mr. Crawford, and Mr. Colin Young.

It is highly probable that of all the terrier tribe, the " Scottie," taken as a whole, is the best companion. He makes a most excellent house-dog, is not too big, does not leave white hairs about all over the place, loves only his master and his master's household, and is, withal, a capable and reliable guard. He is, as a rule, a game, attractive terrier, with heaps of brain power, and from a show point of view there is always some recompense in keeping him, as it will be found he breeds true to type and does not beget offspring of all sorts, shapes, and makes.

Nothing is perfect in this world. Everything has faults. The Scottish Terrier is no exception. His fault is not, however, of his own making. It is a fault which, if possible, should be eradicated, and every step should be taken with a view to accomplishing this. In purchasing a Scottish Terrier one must be careful not to become possessed of one of the timid, nervous, snappy ones. In almost every litter that is born

MR. A. G. COWLEY'S
EMS CAPSULE.

nowadays there is, as a rule, one of this sort. He ought to be put out of the way at once as soon as it is recognised that he belongs to the class, for nothing will ever make him better. He is a degenerate, a result, in the writer's belief, of too much inbreeding. The danger of him is that he is at times the best-looking puppy in the litter, and though it is recognised—after several pounds have been spent on him—that he is no use to show, he is what is called relegated to the stud. The breed is in danger of him, and it is because of the love the writer bears the breed that he begs, in conclusion, for the complete annihilation, root and branch if necessary, of these " dangers."

A Typical Scotch Terrier—Mrs. Hannay's Champion Villain.

THE Scottish Terrier as a show dog dates from about 1877 to 1879. He seems almost at once to have attained popularity, and he has progressed gradually since then, ever in an upward direction, until he is to-day one of the most popular and extensively owned varieties of the dog. Sir Paynton Pigott had, at the date mentioned, a very fine kennel of the breed, for in *The Live Stock Journal* of May 30th, 1879, we find his kennel fully reviewed in a most enthusiastic manner by a correspondent who visited it in consequence of a controversy that was going on at the time, as to whether or not there was such a dog at all, and who, therefore, wished to see and judge for himself as to this point. At the end of his report on the kennel the writer adds these words : " It was certainly one of the happiest days of my life to have the pleasure of looking over so many grand little dogs, but to find them in England quite staggered me. Four dogs and eight bitches are not a bad beginning, and with care and judicious selection in mating, I have little doubt but Mr. Pigott's kennel will be as renowned for Terriers as the late Mr. Laverack's was for Setters. I know but few that take such a delight in the brave little ' die-hards ' as Mr. Pigott, and he may well feel proud of the lot he has got together at great trouble and expense."

The fact that there was such a kennel already in existence proved, of course, a strong point in favour of the *bona fides* of the breed. The best dog in it was Granite, whose portrait and description were given in the *Journal* in connection with the said review ; and the other animals of the kennel being of

Photograph by T. Fall

MRS SPENCER'S DANDIE DINMONT CH. BRAW LAD

A TYPICAL AIREDALE HEAD

the same type, it was at once recognised that there was, in fact, such a breed, and the mouths of the doubters were stopped.

Granite was unquestionably a typical Scottish Terrier, even as we know them at the present day. He was certainly longer in the back than we care for nowadays, and his head also was shorter, and his jaw more snipy than is now seen, but his portrait clearly shows he was a genuine Scottish Terrier, and there is no doubt that he, with his kennel mates, Tartan, Crofter, Syringa, Cavack, and Posey, conferred benefit upon the breed.

To dive deeper into the antiquity of the Scottish Terrier is a thing which means that he who tries it must be prepared to meet all sorts of abuse, ridicule, and criticism. One man will tell you there never was any such thing as the present-day Scottish Terrier, that the mere fact of his having prick ears shows he is a mongrel ; another, that he is merely an offshoot of the Skye or the Dandie ; another, that the only Scottish Terrier that is a Scottish Terrier is a white one ; another, that he is merely a manufactured article from Aberdeen, and so on *ad infinitum*.

It is a most extraordinary fact that Scotland should have unto herself so many different varieties of the terrier. There is strong presumption that they one and all came originally from one variety, and it is quite possible, nay probable, that different crosses into other varieties have produced the assortment of to-day. The writer is strongly of opinion that there still exist in Scotland at the present time specimens of the breed which propagated the lot, which was what is called even now the Highland Terrier, a little long-backed, short-legged, snipy-faced, prick or drop-eared, mostly sandy and black-coloured terrier, game as a pebble, lively as a cricket, and all in all a most, charming little companion ; and further, that to produce our present-day Scottish Terrier— or shall we say, to improve the points of his progenitor ?— the assistance of our old friend the Black and Tan wire-haired terrier of England was sought by a few astute people living probably not very far from Aberdeen.

Scottish Terriers frequently go by the name of Aberdeen Terriers—an appellation, it is true, usually heard only from the lips of people who do not know much about them. Mr. W. L. McCandlish, one of the greatest living authorities on the breed, in an able treatise published some time back, tells us, in reference to this matter, that the terrier under notice went at different periods under the names of Highland, Cairn, Aberdeen, and Scotch ; that he is now known by the proud title of Scottish Terrier ; and that " the only surviving trace of the differing nomenclature is the title Aberdeen, which many people still regard as a different breed—a want of knowledge frequently turned to account by the unscrupulous dealer who is able to sell under the name of Aberdeen a dog too bad to dispose of as a Scottish Terrier." But there can be no doubt that originally there must have been *some* reason for the name. In a letter to the writer, Sir Paynton Pigott says, " Some people call them and advertise them as the Aberdeen Terrier, which is altogether a mistake ; but the reason of it is that forty years ago a Dr. Van Bust, who lived in Aberdeen, bred these terriers to a large extent and sold them, and those buying them called them, in consequence, ' Aberdeen Terriers,' whereas they were in reality merely a picked sort of Old Scotch or Highland Terrier." Sir Paynton himself, as appears from the columns of *The Live Stock Journal* (March 2nd, 1877), bought some of the strain of Van Bust, and therein gives a full description of the same.

Sir Paynton Pigott's kennel of the breed assumed quite large proportions, and was most successful, several times winning all the prizes offered in the variety at different shows. He may well be called the Father of the breed in England, for when he gave up exhibiting, a great deal of his best blood got into the kennels of Mr. H. J. Ludlow, who, as everyone knows, has done such a tremendous amount of good in popularising the breed and has also himself produced such a galaxy of specimens of the very best class. Mr. Ludlow's first terrier was a bitch called Splinter II. The name of Kildee is, in the breed, almost world-famous, and it is interesting to note that in every line does he go back to the said Splinter II. Rambler—called by the great authorities the first pillar of the stud book—was a son of a dog called Bon-Accord, and it is to this latter dog and Roger Rough, and also the aforesaid Tartan and Splinter II. that nearly all of the best present-day pedigrees go back. This being so, it is unnecessary to give many more names of dogs who have in their generations of some years back assisted in bringing the breed to its present state of perfection. An exception, however, must be made in the case of two sons of Rambler, by name Dundee and Alister, names very familiar in the Scottish Terrier pedigrees of the present day. Alister especially was quite an extraordinary stud dog. His progeny were legion, and some very good terriers of to-day own him as progenitor in nearly every line. The best descendants of Alister were Kildee, Tiree, Whinstone, Prince Alexander, and Heather Prince. He was apparently too much inbred to, and though he produced or was responsible for several beautiful terriers, it is much to be doubted whether in a breed which is suffering from the ill-effects of too much inbreeding, he was not one of the greatest sinners.

The Scottish Terrier Club was formed in the year 1882. In the same year a joint committee drew up a standard of perfection for the breed, Messrs. J. B. Morison and Thomson Gray, two gentlemen who were looked upon as great authorities, having a good deal to do with it.

STANDARD OF POINTS OF THE SCOTTISH TERRIER: Skull—Proportionately long, slightly domed and covered with short hard hair about ¼ inch long or less. It should not be quite flat, as there should be a sort of stop or drop between the eyes. Muzzle—Very powerful, and gradually tapering towards the nose, which should always be black and of a good size. The jaws should be perfectly level, and the teeth square, though the nose projects somewhat over the mouth which gives the impression of the upper jaw being longer than the under one. Eyes—A dark-brown or hazel colour ; small, piercing, very bright and rather sunken. **Ears**—Very small, prick or half prick (the former is preferable), but never drop. They should also be sharp pointed, and the hair on them should not be long, but velvety, and they should not be cut. The ears should be free from any fringe at the top. **Neck**—Short, thick and muscular ; strongly set on sloping shoulders. **Chest**—Broad in comparison to the size of the dog, and proportionately deep. **Body**—Of moderate length, but not so long as a Skye's, and rather· flat-sided ; well ribbed up, and exceedingly strong in hind-quarters. **Legs and Feet**—Both fore and hind legs should be short and very heavy in bone, the former being straight and well set on under the body, as the Scottish Terrier should not be out at elbows. The hocks should be bent, and the thighs very muscular, and the feet strong, small and thickly covered with short hair, the fore feet being larger than the hind ones. **Tail**—Should be about 7 inches long, never docked, carried with a slight bend and often gaily. **Coat**—Should be rather short (about 2 inches), intensely hard and wiry in texture, and very dense all over the body. **Size**—From 15 lb. to 20 lb. ; the best weight being as near as possible 18 lb. for-dogs, and 16 lb. for bitches when in condition for work. **Colour**—Steel or iron grey, black brindle, brown brindle, grey brindle, black, sandy and wheaten. White markings are objectionable, and can only be allowed on the chest and to a small extent. **General Appearance**—The face should wear a very sharp, bright and active expression, and the head should be carried up. The dog (owing to the shortness of his coat) should appear to be higher on the leg than he really is ; but at the same time he should look compact and possessed of great muscle in his hind-quarters. In fact, a Scottish Terrier, though essentially a terrier, cannot be too powerfully put together, and should be from about 9 inches ·to 12 inches in height.

SPECIAL FAULTS : Muzzle—Either under or over hung. **Eyes**—Large or light-coloured. **Ears**—Large, round at the points or drop. It is also a fault if they are too heavily covered with hair. **Legs**—Bent, or slightly bent, and out at elbows. **Coat**—Any silkiness, wave or tendency to curl is a serious blemish, as is also an open coat. **Size**—Specimens of over 20 lb. should be discouraged.

There have, of recent years, been many very excellent specimens of the Scottish Terrier bred and exhibited. Pre-eminent among them stands Mrs. Hannay's Ch. Heworth Rascal, who was a most symmetrical terrier, and probably the nearest approach to perfection in the breed yet seen. Other very first-class terriers have been the same lady's Ch. Gair, Mr. Powlett's Ch. Callum Dhu, Mr. McCandlish's Ems Cosmetic, Mr. Chapman's Heather Bob and Heather Charm, Mr. Kinnear's Seafield Rascal, Mr. Wood's Hyndman Chief, Messrs. Buckley and Mills's Clonmel Invader, and Mr. Deane Willis's Ch. Huntley Daisy and Ch. Carter Laddie.

It is highly probable that of all the terrier tribe, the

"Scottie," taken as a whole, is the best companion. He makes a most excellent house-dog, is not too big, does not leave white hairs about all over the place, loves only his master and his master's household, and is, withal, a capable and reliable guard. He is, as a rule, a game, attractive terrier, with heaps of brain power, and from a show point of view there is always some recompense in keeping him, as it will be found he breeds true to type and does not beget offspring of all sorts, shapes, and makes.

SCOTTISH TERRIERS.

It is a custom of many people to condemn dog shows as causing the production of a wrong type of dog for use or companionship. It would be out of place to examine the truth, or otherwise, of this contention, but undisputed credit must be given to dog shows for the introduction and popularity of many breeds which would hardly be known had there been no dog shows and no stimulant to their production. As compared with the passing generation, the dog-lover of to-day has a very much wider choice of breeds from which to select the dog whose characteristics of appearance, utility or disposition best suit his requirements. Many breeds popular five-and-twenty years ago are rarely to be met with now, and other breeds then unknown, except to a few, have taken their place. In some degree it is cause for regret that old breeds should disappear or even decay, and where the decline is due to fashion's decree in desiring the latest thing, the cause and the result are both to be deplored ; but in some instances breeds of dogs have steadily fought their way into popularity and have routed their competitors under the primary laws of the survival of the fittest. Among such breeds a prominent example is the Scottish Terrier.

ROGER ROUGH.   (1876).

A short-legged, rough-coated breed of terrier is known to have existed in the mountainous regions of Scotland for some hundreds of years. The type of these dogs varied considerably, and three or four of the breeds recognised under distinct names by the Kennel Club owe their origin to this highland terrier of Scotland. It has been contended by some that the points now desired by exhibitors of such breeds have been produced artificially by continued selection, but when we consider the short period during which they have been influenced by show competition, it is conceding too much to the skill

"REGINA." (1886).

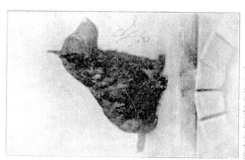

Photo by Knight, Kettering.
"SCOTCH REEL." (1891).

"EMS COSMETIC." (1903).

"TIBER." (1889).

100

of breeders that the modern champion dog of these breeds could be as he is unless his pre-show-day ancestors had possessed among them the various features which, in correct combination, led to the title. It is affirmed by modern scientists, who have made a special study of heredity, that man cannot force Nature, but only follow her lead. We must, therefore, believe that among the various types of the highland terrier there were individuals possessed of the features of the breeds now known as the Scottish, Skye and West Highland White Terrier. It would serve no purpose to endeavour to prove that one of these types was the original from which the others are variations, for positive proof is impossible. It may be argued, on the one hand, that there is natural tendency towards a short-skulled and snipey-faced type, and, on the other hand, that as there is no breed possessed of such large teeth for the size of dog, nor such long skulls, these could not have been obtained by an outcross with another breed ; and as the early show-bench dogs possessed long heads and big teeth, it was not continued selection for exhibition that produced them. We may assume from this, with reasonable certainty, that dogs possessed of the features of present-day winning Scottish Terriers existed long before shows had any influence on the breed, and the chief effect shows have had is that breeders have aimed at, and occasionally succeeded in, combining in one animal all the best features found in the early highland terriers. It is known that exhibitors of some of the earliest dogs shown, such as Sir Paynton Pigott and Captain Mackie, were able to select from scores of highland dogs only a very few which were regarded as sufficiently good to exhibit and breed from.

The original terrier was kept for fox-killing purposes, but the number of dogs required for this object is very limited, and the growth in numbers of the Scottish Terrier is not due to any pronounced excellence over other breeds in this respect. The rapid increase in their popularity is due to something else than their ability to enter a fox's earth or scramble through rocky cairns, and it is hypocrisy to contend that pedigree dogs are bred for this purpose. At the same time, the dog's ability to work, and his build for the peculiarities of his work, went to the making of his character and his general appearance. If breeders lose sight of the foundation stones on which the breed was formed they will soon build up a wrong structure and the breed will lose its individual appearance and the idiosyncrasies of its character, and with them will go all the charm and fascination.

It is the peculiar character more than the peculiar appearance of Scottish Terriers that has won for them countless devotees. "Devotee" is the right word to use, for once anyone has owned a Scottish Terrier possessed of the genuine character all other breeds of dogs are regarded as merely dogs, while the Scottish Terrier is a personality. He may have taken upon himself the outward appear-

BONACCORD. (about 1879).

ance of a dog, and the biologist may classify him as such, but those who have close acquaintance with him know that the outward form is a deception, and that within is a spirit more human than dog-like. It would seem as though a gallant and noble-minded race of men had been condemned for some cause to inhabit the frame of a dog, and in a Scottish Terrier's eyes, especially as they grow older, there is a look, somewhat sad, which seems to ask, "Cannot you see that I understand as you understand ; that my feelings are as your feelings ; that I am as you are, except that I am condemned to take this shape

102

and be confined to the communicative restrictions of a dog, but cannot you find some way of really knowing all I tell you, and of conveying to me all your desires?" To some people it is difficult to understand why anyone should like to own half-a-dozen or more dogs. One or even two seem to them pleasant chattels, but half-a-dozen is over-doing a good thing. Such people cannot be properly acquainted with Scottish Terriers, for each individual has an entirely distinct personality, and it is as reasonable to argue that no man ought to have more than two friends as it is to restrict one's canine friends to so small a number. Where each terrier has a distinct individuality,

" Ch. Dundee." (1882).

a number adds interest, and does not detract from the amount of friendship given to each.

One cause of the attractions of the breed is that they are not fussy nor too demonstrative. They take a very philosophic view of life, and are quick to make distinctions between people. They show good manners towards your acquaintances, and are prepared to be friends with your friends, but palpably accepting them for your sake. They take the best of life when it comes ; they make the best of life as they find it. They have a sturdy independence, and yet wholehearted, unselfish devotion. They are not necessarily quick at learning tricks, such, in truth, bore them. They have too much sense—perhaps too much appreciation of their own worth—to care to learn merely to " show off," and their woe-begone countenance when being taught, while amusing, is expressive of their feeling that they are being asked to do something nonsensical. They will learn when they see that to do so will please their human friends, but they do so after protest.

While all Scottish Terriers have this peculiarly human character, it is not contended that all have it in the same degree, and, as in the human race there are many fools and others who suffer in different

WHINSTONE. (1888).

but analogous ways, so also there are Scottish Terriers which have defects in their natures. The most common form is in a shyness to the human, similar to that possessed by all wild animals, and this and other traits recur from time to time in individual specimens to remind us of the lonely life their ancestors led among the Scottish moors, where the whistling of the wind down the glens and the eerie cry of the peewit on the moorlands filled the Keltic imagination with tales of sprites and elfins, of death warnings, and the converse of spirits.

Though in an Encyclopædia it may seem beside the point to write in this strain of a breed; the really important matter in connection with the breed is the distinction in character between it and other breeds of terriers. Something, however, must be mentioned of the form of the animal, and in this, too, it has its idiosyncrasies. The prick ears, the long, keen face, the short legs, and the peculiar bear-like walk give a quaint, old-fashioned air. There are some who count a Scottish Terrier ugly, and it may be, in the words of the Irishman, that to admire him is an acquired taste like heaven, but the poet has more truly said:

" Oh beauteous is creation in fashion and device ;
If I have failed to find thee fair, 'tis blindness is my vice."

The Scottish Terrier should convey in his form the combination of strength and activity. His legs should be short and the body placed low upon them, as it is important for balance that the centre of gravity be low, and his natural work over boulders and along rocky ledges necessitates balance. To give activity and jumping ability the loin must be strongly knit, the hind-quarters big, and the stifle well bent ; the shoulders should slope, and the point where the blades meet behind the neck should be high. The tail is not merely an appendage, and only required for wagging, but is of great practical use. Many desire a short tail, but this is a fancy point founded on the fashion of docked tails in other breeds, and has no real justification. On the contrary, it ought to be of fair length and very thick at the root, giving the impression of forming a very useful balancing pole. Once this idea is grasped, a very short or a thin tail is an eyesore. It should be straight, and carried, as a rule, fairly upright, and if, at times of great excitement, it is raised higher than the perpendicular, it may be an excusable fault, but none the less a fault, and when the tail points distinctly forward it is a most serious defect. The body is big for the size of dog, the ribs widely sprung across the back, and flattening as they descend into a deep chest. The brisket should be prominent. The skull is long, moderately broad, or, to avoid misconception, call it, if you will, moderately narrow, with clean cheeks, while the muzzle is of less length and tapering towards the nose, which is of fair size and not snipey. In prints and photographs of old dogs there is only short hair on the muzzle, but modern taste has desired what is called more " furnishing " on the foreface. This adds

105

a little to the generally conceived idea of terrier expression, and in itself there is no objection to it, but it is very rarely that dogs with much hair on the muzzle have the proper hard coat on the skull and body, and as it is a fancy point and a taste which can easily be changed, it would be better if there was a reversion to the taste for short, hard hair on the foreface, and less was heard of powerful muzzles, which, as a rule, prove to be only much be-whiskered faces. Much whisker is often of considerable value in the show ring, for

Ch. Gair. (1895).

more people are deceived by hair when judging than is casually understood. The hair on the skull should be short and hard, but the whiskered dog seldom possesses this short, hard hair, so most dogs are shown without any hard hair on the skull. It is a question of fashion more than fancy, but the correct thing is unquestionably the short, hard hair on all parts of the head. The body coat is longer, but also hard and close. There are in reality two coats, one very short and dense and soft, the other longer and much harder, and also dense. The eyes are moderate in size. A small eye, like a rough fox terrier's, is too small for a Scottish Terrier, but the latter's should not appear either large or full. It should be set under the skull bone, but not deeply, and it should be almond-shaped. In colour the best is a rich, dark hazel, distinctly brown in tone and not black. The ears are carried erect, pointed and free from fringe of hair; in size they should be moderate. Ears too large are the common fault, but ears too small are equally disfiguring. The standard for the breed admirably sums up the general appearance.

CH. HEWORTH BANTOCK. (1904).

"The face should wear a very sharp, bright, and active expression, and the head should be carried up. The dog (owing to the shortness of his coat) should appear to be higher on the leg than he really is; but, at the same time, he should look compact, and possessed of great muscle in his hind-quarters. In fact, the Scottish Terrier, though essentially a terrier, cannot be too powerfully put together, and should be from 9in. to 12in. in height."

In conformity with the custom in other breeds of terriers, there has been a recent fashion for straight forelegs. This fashion has led to breeders selecting for exhibition and reproductive purposes Scottish Terriers with straight legs, even when they possessed other undesirable features. Dogs with straight fronts have, almost invariably, been such as are higher on the leg than the terrier of fifteen and more years ago. As a rule, they have been lighter in bone, with thin feet; the shoulders have been too straight, the bodies flat-sided, and not sufficient bend at the stifle. When a point makes such radical changes on a type of dog, there must be something fundamentally wrong with it, unless we are to say that lowness to ground, good bone and feet, sloping shoulders, spring of rib and bent stifles are of secondary importance to a straight front. To argue so might be to argue in favour of a nice dog, but it would not be a Scottish Terrier. The truth is that breeders and judges have shown weakness in upholding their own breed and have bowed the head to the dictates of exhibitors and judges of a very different breed and breeds of terriers. It should be understood and recognised once and for all that the Scottish Terrier ought to be placed on his legs low to the ground, and that this placement necessitates very different construction to the breeds of more leggy terriers. If this is recognised straightness of front will be relegated to its proper position, and that position would be that where a dog possessed correct make and shape, good bone, sloping shoulders, big heart room and lung space, great quarters, strong loin and well bent stifles, he might be none the worse for a straight front. To put it in this way—without being prejudiced against a straight front, the writer has never seen a straight front on a dog possessing the features here mentioned and doubts if the combination is possible, and even if it is possible, it is very questionable that anyone would like it when seen. The forelegs of a Scottish terrier ought not to be constructed like a hound's; for one thing, the leg is too short to combine a sloping shoulder with straight pasterns, and obtain liberty of action. The feet should be turned slightly outwards; there ought to be a slight bend outwards at the pastern; the elbows should be parallel to each other, and the humerus should be sufficiently sloped outwards from the brisket to allow the chest to

108

come between the elbows, without any suggestion that the dog is out at shoulder. The chief point to observe in this description is the pastern. If a bent pastern is recommended, people recall the dogs of long ago, whose pasterns were so bent as to touch each other. A bend in the line of the leg at the pastern does not imply weakness in itself. It is only when carried to excess that the dog becomes unsound. The type of leg advocated is only a very slight bend, and admittedly it is advocated, solely and only, in order to obtain the best

" CH. KEPPOCH DUGALD." (1908).

form of forehand, of body and of quarters. It is every bit as sound as a straight front, and it means correct formation of every other part of the dog.

Importance has been given to the question of forelegs—or "front," as it is commonly called—because the general structure of the dog varies with it. A tendency of dog-showing is that certain points, in themselves desirable, are developed into fetishes, and become the stock-in-trade of the man with limited knowledge but unlimited self-assurance. Anyone, unless defective in sight, can see if a front is straight, a back is short, and a head long and narrow, and on the basis of such phrases he can place dogs in order at a show with plausible reasons for his judgment. It requires a little knowledge of anatomy and an eye for shape, line and symmetry to judge animals with the object of deciding which of them is constructed in the best way for the work it has to do. A dog with a long, narrow head, a straight front, a short body and tail, a harsh coat, dark eyes and prick ears is not of necessity a good Scottish Terrier. Many of the dogs of recent years possessed of these features have been nice looking terriers, but

"Ch. Nosegay Forget-me-not."

they have not been good Scottish Terriers. A good Scottish Terrier may have a straight front, and is probably the better for having a body moderately short, but the reason why so few good Scottish Terriers have been seen lately is that straight fronts and short bodies have been the fashionable shibboleth among breeders, exhibitors and judges, and however much better a dog may have been in other respects it had to go below a flat-sided, quarterless, boneless, thin-footed, jumped-up creature, possessed of straight forelegs and with a body, such as it was, short in length. The craze extends to such a ridiculous extent that breeders will not use a terrier unless it possesses these two points, and shape and make and Scottish Terrier character and expression are left to look after themselves.

The writer is well aware it is more easy to write condemning a practice than to set up a new one or even avoid the old practice, though aware of its shortcomings. The present and future of a breed is in the keeping of those who breed for and attend shows, and show-goers discuss among themselves the points of the breed, the merits and defects of well-known terriers, and, not unnaturally, the trend of all exhibitors is towards a fixed groove. It is well, therefore, to endeavour now and again to get outside show-going and show influence in order to look at the direction the prevailing taste, or

A MODERN HEAD.

fashion, among show-goers is driving the breed, and compare it with the type formed in one's own mind as the ideal. If this is not done a breeder will whisk about to each puff of fashion's changeable wind, and consistent breeding is then impossible. There will always be a tendency to exaggeration where keen competition exists, and it is necessary to counteract this exaggeration from time to time, and to direct attention to the reason why some feature is required of a particular make in order that breeders may perceive that perfection lies in moderation and that excess either way is a fault. To prevent distorted importance being placed on forelegs and short bodies it would be well to give up the slip-shod habit of speaking about straight fronts and short bodies, and speak rather of sound forelegs and strongly-coupled bodies. This phraseology would not imply that it was a straight front or short body that was wanted, but sound legs and feet and muscular, well-knit bodies. A muscular, well-knit body is, necessarily, somewhat short, and, therefore, fulfils the requirements of the dog much more than "short body," which might, and not infrequently does, possess neither the requisite substance and muscle, nor the required liberty of movement and powerful propelling quarters. If the reason why certain points are desired is borne in mind, and not merely the description of the point, we shall have our dogs judged on more thoughtful and general lines, and the breed will steadily revert to the sturdy, independent customer he once was, and in some instances still is. The material exists, and if encouragement is given to breeders to make a strong effort to reproduce it, it will quickly reassert itself.

THE ILLUSTRATIONS.

"Roger Rough, 1876."

Roger Rough (K.C.S.B. 10938), born 1876, by Fury ex Flo—owner, Mr. J. A. Adamson.

This is one of the dogs from which almost every present-day pedigreed Scottish Terrier descends. He was owned by Mr. Adamson, of Aberdeen, one of the pioneers of the breed, who still occasionally exhibits, and almost more rarely judges. In an old advertisement Mr. Adamson describes the dog as 16½lbs. in weight, which is considerably less than the weight given in the standard, issued in 1881, and still retained ; so he probably was rather smaller than the average dog of his own day. The dog seems to want substance, according to our taste, and the head seems short, though excellent in expression.

"Bonaccord, about 1879."

Bonaccord (K.C.S.B. 12051), birth and pedigree unknown—exhibited, 1881.

Owned originally by Mr. Adamson, he became the property of Messrs. Ludlow and Blomfield. The mating of Bonaccord with Mr. Ludlow's Splinter II. produced Ch. Rambler, Ch. Tatters II., and other terriers that are the groundwork of every living terrier. Mr. Ludlow, more than any other breeder, helped to make the breed popular in England, and for a great number of years he was Honorary Secretary of the Scottish Terrier Club, England.

The photograph of Bonaccord does not impress the modern breeder, and he looks both short in head and rather leggy.

112

" Ch. Dundee, 1882."

Dundee (K.C.S.B. 16818), born 1882, by Rambler ex Worry—breeders, Messrs. Ludlow and Blomfield.

First exhibited by Captain Mackie, this dog had a remarkable show career, winning at the Scottish Kennel Club Show from 1884 to 1889. As the photograph shows, this is more like the modern type than the previous pictures—longer in head and more massive in body. There is no doubt he was regarded in his own day as a distinct improvement on anything that had been seen before, although he was not an alteration in type. He was merely the combination in one dog of desirable features possessed by the breed in the past. It will be noticed that the head tapered more towards the nose than modern taste deems correct, but the tapering face gave a keen, enquiring expression many modern dogs lack. The size of eye is also to be remarked, as the Scottish Terrier's eye in size takes a medium place between such breeds as the fox terrier and the Dandie Dinmont. Captain Mackie owned a strong kennel in the eighties, and toured more than once through the Highlands in search of good terriers.

" Regina, 1886."

Regina (K.C.S.B. 21436), born 1886, by Tuath, ex Midge, by Durcara—breeder, Mr. A. O. Mudie.

This bitch shares with her ancestor, Splinter II., breeding honours in the development of the modern Scottish Terrier. To give a list of her descendants would be to name more than half the winning dogs of the past 20 years, but descended in tail female from her we get such stud dogs as Ch. Rascal, Ch. Heather Bob and Ems Tonic. It is of interest to compare the head of Regina with that of Whinstone, showing a difference for long maintained by the Seafield and Heather blood respectively. Regina was acquired early in her life by Mr. J. N. Reynard, and had much to do with the fame of his kennel. In the last few years he has not shown as much as formerly, but he still takes an active interest in the breed. For many years he acted as Honorary Secretary of the Scottish Terrier Club, Scotland, and is now President, and his energy has had much to do with the position the breed holds to-day.

" Whinstone, 1888."

Whinstone (K.C.S.B. 27897), born 1888, by Ch. Alister, ex Heather Belle—breeder, Mr. J. F. Alexander.

Though a fairly successful show dog, Whinstone's claim to post-humous honours depends on the link he forms between the great stud dogs, Ch. Alister and Heather Prince, and in the birth of the latter being due to the mating of Prince Alexander to Heather Bee, the one being his son and the other his litter sister.

113

"Tiree, 1889."

Tiree (K.C.S.B. 30061), born 1889, by Ch. Alister, ex Coll—breeder, Captain Wetherall.

This dog won first in open class at Edinburgh two years in succession, after close fights with Ch. Rascal, and the illustration is of value as showing a good bodied dog of 20 years ago. His head was rather short, and his eye light enough ; while his legs were straight, they were placed too much under the body. Captain Wetherall was for many years a successful breeder with a very limited kennel. He was greatly respected as an exhibitor, and had a keen knowledge of the breed.

"Scotch Reel, 1891."

Scotch Reel (K.C.S.B. 35074), born 1891, by Ch. Rascal, ex Rea— Tiree's sister—breeder, Capt. Wetherall.

This bitch was the best Scottish Terrier Captain Wetherall ever bred, and comes into the select list of those that have claims to be considered the best ever bred. As will be seen, she had a head of the Regina type, and the ears are carried more forward on the skull than the ideal. She was a small bitch of good substance, and the muzzle was deep without the aid of whiskers.

"Ch. Gair, 1895."

Gair (K.C.S.B. 1210 A), born 1895, by Heather Prince, ex Rustic Beauty—breeder, Mr. W. Marshall.

The fame of Mrs. Hannay's kennel may be said to commence from the purchase of this dog for a figure deemed high in those days. Mrs. Hannay's part in the annals of the Scottish Terrier breed fall to be recorded by a later historian, as she is still an active exhibitor, lightening the trials of dog-showing by her good humour. Gair was a dog with an excellent body, beautifully placed upon his legs. His head could with advantage have been a little longer, but he was a grand dog of a very good type.

"Ch. Ems Cosmetic, 1903."

Ems Cosmetic (K.C.S.B. 1504 J), born 1903, by Ems Tonic, ex Ch. Seafield Beauty—breeder, Mr. W. L. McCandlish.

The painting, from which this illustration is a reproduction, is by Mr. Arthur Wardle, and is an excellent portrait. It shows off the features of this bitch so well that further remark is unnecessary. Others, besides her owner, consider that she, too, has claims for consideration as the best of all time.

"Ch. Heworth Bantock, 1904."

Heworth Bantock (K.C.S.B. 1357 K), born 1904, by Ems Tonic, ex Ems Bhanavar—breeder, Mr. W. L. McCandlish.

This is another purchase of Mrs. Hannay's that has been led by her to fame. The illustration shows a long-headed dog and very typical body.

114

" Ch. Keppoch Dugald, 1908."

Keppoch Dugald (K.C.S.B. 738 P), born 1908, by West Point Piper, ex Karla Maisie—breeder, Mr. T. W. MacDonald.

This dog brings the illustrations down to date as that of the most successful dog of the present day. He is another example of the low-to-ground, sturdy terrier. Mr. Macdonald has bred Scottish Terriers for a number of years, and has been remarkably successful with a kennel that seldom contains as many as six terriers, and more usually only a couple of brood bitches. His is an example of what can be done without embarking on large numbers, and his success must act as an incentive to those whose circumstances make the reduction of numbers to a minimum a necessity.

" Ch. Nosegay Forget-me not," American.

Nosegay Forget-me-not is the first American bred champion, though from English parentage, being by Loyne Ruffian, ex Ringlet, by Ch. Revival, ex Charybdis—breeder, Dr. F. C. Ewing.

" A modern head."

This is a portrait of a typical head of the exaggerated sort. The proportions of the skull and muzzle are good, and the eye well placed.

W. L. McCANDLISH

115

SCOTCH TERRIER

SCOTCH TERRIER
(SHOWING HEAD AND FRONT.) THE CORRECT TYPE OF HEAD; EARS;
CARRIAGE OF STERN AND GENERAL CONFIGURATION ARE WELL DISPLAYED

117

SCOTCH TERRIER. (PROFILE VIEW)

118

THE SCOTTISH TERRIER

Scottish Terriers, incorrectly known as Aberdeens,* are a breed which you must care for if you care for dogs at all. They have become more domesticated and more human-like than many others, and are very affectionate and independent. They are very alert and decidedly active when needs be.

The colours are various ; greys, black, sand, and brindles. The blacks are perhaps the favourite. Dogs weigh about 18 lb ; bitches a pound or two less. They stand from nine to twelve inches from the ground.

At one time they were bred too large, and care is now taken to keep the size in check ; a strong, stocky little fellow is needed.

Short, level body and great bone, pricked ears, square jaws, and very dark eyes, are characters which make the breed. The harsh dense overcoat covers a soft coat below. At Edinburgh there is a monument to a Scotch Terrier ' Bobby,' who remained by the grave of its owner for fourteen years, fed by a local restaurant-keeper. Bobby died in 1872.

*This name applied to broken-haired, prick-eared terriers weighing 8 to 25 lb, which ran in streets of Aberdeen in 1887. (*Vide* D. J. T. GRAY).

1

2

THE SCOTTISH TERRIER

It has always been the endeavour of owners of varieties to attempt to make a breed conform with an ideal, and to give to it the shape, size, texture of coat, or other characteristics considered an improvement, and consequently to be desired. So was it, that the *Terrier of Scotland*, the *Cairn*, by skilful breeding and selection, and by breeders always keeping the desired type in mind, was altered to make the most attractive variety known as the Scottish Terrier. It is of interest to note that this happened in the towns, and it is doubtful if those, who first of all exhibited the breed, would have been able to give an accurate account of the actual breeding that had gone to make it, the ancestry going back to the time when pedigree was unthought of and indiscriminate breeding usual.[2] It is now over a hundred years since the type that was claimed to be the *Scottish Terrier* first attracted notice. The country-side Cairn Terriers, working, rough-coated Terriers, were relegated into the same category as the wire-haired Terriers in England. In the towns a Cairn-like Terrier, with certain alterations from the original type, had attracted attention. It was therefore to be expected that the owners of the improved variety considered it justifiable to name the variety the Scottish Terrier. It was early days, but the type was already fixed. The name was the difficulty. Terriers born on the soil of Scotland, of ancestry decidedly native, were imagined, not unnaturally, to be the desired Scottish Terrier. In Yorkshire and in other parts of England " Scottish Terriers," as they were termed, were exhibited. They won prizes, the judges taking the word of the exhibitor as to the nature of the variety. Whilst such was the state of affairs, a type of Cairn Terrier had been fixed, which may be said to have been the old type of Cairn with but slight alterations. In 1868 Scottish Terriers were exhibited at Craven Show, in Yorkshire. Scottish Terriers were a usual class. At some shows, Scottish Terrier classes contained so many different types that the judges were unable to decide which

[1] Her Majesty Queen Victoria had, it is stated, a pair of West Highland White Terriers presented to her by the Duke of Argyll. This probably is incorrect, and may refer to Skye Terriers.

[2] Youatt, in 1845, gives an illustration of long-legged, rough-coated dog as a Scottish Terrier, and describes the breed to be of no particular type.

breed was the breed to which the title *Scottish Terrier* had been applied.[1] In 1879 a class for the breed was given at the Kennel Club Show. It was anticipated that similar difficulty would be experienced. The anticipation proved wrong. Fifteen entries appeared, and these dogs were one and all of the same type and of the nature of the *present-day Scottish Terrier*, except that they were not so stocky nor so good on their legs. At the show a dog named *Otter*[2] won first prize.

We can appreciate the confusion when we are informed that at one show *Otter* appeared in two classes—that for the *Scottish Terrier* breed, and that for the Skye Terrier, winning in both classes! It was the commencement of the present-day Scottish Terrier, for the interest aroused in *Otter* and similar dogs, the meeting of owners and, later, the breeding together of some of the exhibits, laid the foundation of the variety on a firmer basis. It was now fully understood what constituted a Scottish Terrier. From the day of the show owners of Scottish Terriers had drawn aside. It was recognised that these Terriers did indeed constitute a distinct variety. *Whinstone*, the editor of the *Scottish Fancier*, decided to ascertain the origin of the breed, and Captain Mackie started on his journeys. Once he thought he had discovered them at a croft " where a short-petticoated, red-armed, tousie-headed lass " told him that he would find the real thing in a shed she pointed out to him. This happened at the home of the old fox-hunter, to whom I have alluded in my notes on the Cairn breed. So Captain Mackie returned. He had found no Scottish Terrier, but had formed the opinion that the *Scottish Terrier* had been made from the *foxy-headed vermin dogs* or *hard-haired-Highlands*, the *Cairn*.[3]

Whilst such developments were taking place a further variety appeared, described to be distinct ; to be the *Aberdeen*. Its appearance was viewed with much displeasure. At the instigation of a breeder a class was arranged for the breed. The classes proved unsatisfactory : the judge who had offered the prizes refused to give them. Aberdeen was a centre for Scottish Terriers. Many were kept and bred there and left that city for homes further south.

Moreover, the name Aberdeen being easier to say than Scottish Terrier, the name Aberdeen was generally adopted. Breeders of Scottish Terriers insisted that the breed was no *Aberdeen*, but the Scottish Terrier. Hugh Dalziel,[4] much to their disgust, wrote in his work that he would call them *Aberdeens*—ascribing them as *short-legged Aberdonians*. But he was soon to change his mind, for in the next edition of his work he writes that " as long as we get Scotch collops from Scotch bullocks, and Scotch whisky to aid the digestion of the collops, we may surely have Scotch Terriers." But his change of opinion came too late ; the name *Aberdeen* had become

[1] At the Crystal Palace Show of 1875 there was one entry, the only dog exhibited as a Scottish Terrier, a rough-haired black-and-tan, " which could not find a purchaser for 10s." At the Brighton Show of 1876 there were two entries in the Scottish Terrier class, one described as "a rough-haired Terrier and a poor specimen," the other as a Yorkshire Terrier.

[2] See Plate 8, No. 21.

[3] *Whinstone*, in his report of the journey, states that in his opinion the long-legged Scottish Terrier had died out in Scotland, but that the Irish Terriers was exactly similar to the long-legged Scottish Terrier.

[4] Dalziel, in his book, writes : " The old hard and short-haired ' terry ' of the West of Scotland, as I recollected him, was a dog much nearer in shape to a modern Fox-terrier, but with a short and rounder head." See also *Stonehenge's* Scottish Terrier, Plate 26, No. 3.

fixed in the public mind, and has remained in constant use, whilst the right and proper title of the variety is the Scottish Terrier.[1]

In 1882 a club was formed. We find *Whinstone* (Mr. Thomas Gray) one of the vice-presidents, and Mr. Krehl the other, and Captain Mackie and also Mr. H. J. Ludlow, as members. Mr. J. B. Morrison, who judged at the 1879 show, was the president of the Club. Later Mr. Morrison drew up the standard of Scottish Terriers, a standard which has remained in force with but few alterations since.

From the days of *Otter* the breed has been constantly improved.[2] To-day it is a stocky, short-legged little dog. *Hyndman Chief*, born in 1893, was considered a dog of remarkable type. He won eighty first prizes, and stood at stud at the then high fee of £3 3s. His photograph could be obtained for 2s. To-day *Hyndman Chief* would have little chance, even at one of the smaller shows, to win a card of any kind at all! A remarkably beautiful Scottish Terrier now appeared, *Kildee*, the property of the well-known Mr. Ludlow, an old-established breeder and authority. *Kildee*, a champion, won over one hundred first prizes, and his value as a sire can be appreciated when we know that he was the father of more than forty winning show dogs. *Kildee* went back to Mr. Ludlow's first Scottish Terrier, *Splinter II.*, often termed "the mother of the Scottish Terrier breed."

The Scottish Terrier breed was popular. Good prices were reported. Mr. J. E. Smith, the St. Bernard breeder and owner of *Save*, claimed *Glory* at Birmingham Show at £110, and later bought from Mr. J. N. Reynard *Clydeford Rebal* at £150. Among the leading owners of Scottish Terriers were Mr. R. Chapman, of Glenboig ; Mr. Kinnear, of Kirkaldy, and Mrs. Hannay, of Heworth Hall. Mr. Chapman sold *Heather Nellie* for over £200, and later Mr. Chapman's son refused £200 for his dog *Tosker*. Mrs. Hannay bought from Mr. Kinnear his *Seafield Prince* for £250, and changed his name to *Heworth Rascal*. At the time Mrs. Hannay bought the dog, I think her noted Ch. *Gair*, a celebrity in the town of Dundee, was recently deceased. In 1902 one of the best classes for Scottish Terriers that has ever been seen was staged at Edinburgh Show. There were seventy-three dogs present, the most important dogs of the breed, including *Revival* (so named because he was reared by hand, his mother dying on whelping). The class was won by Mrs. Hannay's purchase, *Heworth Rascal*, *Revival* standing second. Two Scottish Terriers of remarkable type at that time were *Romany Duchess* and *Romany Risca*. Later new names appeared amongst the leaders controlling the destinies of the variety : Mr. J. Deane Willis, whose prefix was *Bapton*, and Mr. W. L. McCandlish, whose prefix was *Ems*, and the late Mr. H. R. B. Tweed, whose dogs had the prefix of Laindon, a corner of Essex, where Mr. Tweed resided.[3] The *Albourne* dogs, the property of Mr. A. G. Cowley, and the *Laurieston* dogs, the property of Mr. W. Davidson, the Ornsay kennel of Mr. J. Campbell, and Mr. Ferrier's *Taybank* dogs, are some of the most important Scottish Terrier kennels in history.

The development of interest in the Scottish breed may be seen from

---

[1] Mr. William Lort had suggested that some rough-haired Terriers he had judged should be named *Aberdeens*. Later, I believe at his instigation, a class for *Aberdeens* was put on at Birmingham show, the prizes, so it is stated, being offered by Mr. Lort, a matter to which I have alluded

[2] Captain Mackie's Scottish Terriers are described to have stood 10 in. high, to have been 17 in. to 18 in. round the chest. The dog of to-day stands 9 in. to 12 in. from the ground.

[3] The late Mr. Tweed's favourite champion, *Laindon Lumen.* See Plate 26, No. 7.

the following statistics, giving the variety registered in the years 1914 and 1915, and 1922 to 1930 :—

	Skyes.	Cairns.	West Highland White.	Scottish.	Total Terriers of Scotland registered.
1914	19	191	631	600	1,441
1915	38	204	522	573	1,337
1922	18	572	371	812	1,773
1923	31	727	499	888	2,145
1924	50	803	587	1,352	2,792
1925	40	1,266	688	1,437	3,431
1926	71	1,502	758	1,648	3,979
1927	58	1,745	721	1,804	4,328
1928	48	1,986	715	1,917	4,666
1929	46	2,223	726	2,005	5,000
1930	62	2,312	663	2,190	5,227
Total for 11 years	481	13,531	6,881	15,226	36,119

THE SCOTTISH TERRIER.

Skull : Proportionately long, slightly domed, and covered with short hard hair, about ¾ inch long, or less.   It should not be quite flat, as there should be a distinct stop, or drop, between the eyes. **Muzzle :** Very powerful, and gradually tapering towards the nose. Nose black, and of a good size. The jaws perfectly level and the teeth square, though the nose projects somewhat over the mouth, which gives the impression of the upper jaw being longer than the under one. **Eyes :** A dark brown or hazel colour; small, piercing, very bright, and rather sunken. **Ears :** Small and erect, sharp-pointed, and the hair on them not long but velvety, and they should not be cut. The ears should be free from any fringe at the top. **Neck :** Short, thick and muscular ; strongly set on sloping shoulders. **Chest :** Broad in comparison to the size of the dog, and proportionately deep. **Body :** Of moderate length and rather flat-sided, well ribbed up, and exceedingly strong in hindquarters. Both **fore and hind legs** short and very heavy in bone, the former appearing straight, and well set on under the body, as the Scotch Terrier should not be out at elbows. The hocks should be bent, and the thighs very muscular ; and the feet strong, small and thickly covered with short hair, the **forefeet** being larger than the hind ones. **Tail :** Not more than 7 inches long, **never docked,** carried with a slight bend, and often gaily. **Coat :** Of two textures, the outer intensely hard and wiry in texture, and the under, short, soft and exceedingly dense. **Size :** From 15 lb. to 20 lb., the best weight being as near as possible 18 lb. for dogs, and 16 lb. for bitches, when in condition. **Colour :** Steel or iron grey, black-brindle, brown-brindle, grey-brindle, black, sandy, and wheaten. White markings are objectionable, and can only be allowed on the chest, and to a small extent. **General :** The face wears a very sharp, bright and active expression, and the head is carried up. The dog (owing to the shortness of his coat) appears to be higher on the leg than he really is ; but at the same time, looks compact, and possessed of great muscle in his hindquarters. A Scottish Terrier, though essentially a Terrier, cannot be too powerfully put together, and should be from 9 inches to 12 inches in height. **Faults : Muzzle**—Either under or over-hung. **Eyes :** Large or light colour. **Ears :** Large, round at the points, or drop. It is also a fault if they are too heavily covered with hair. **Legs :** Bent or slightly bent, and out at elbows. **Coat :** Any silkiness, wave, or tendency to curl is a serious blemish, as is also an open coat. **Size :** Over 20 lb. should be discouraged.

	POINTS.
Skull	$7\frac{1}{2}$
Muzzle	$7\frac{1}{2}$
Eyes	5
Ears	5
Neck	5
Chest	5
Body	15
Legs and feet	10
Tail	$2\frac{1}{2}$
Coat	15
Size	10
Colour	$2\frac{1}{2}$
General appearance	10
Total	100

126

Photo]   [Hedges, Lytham
SCOTTISH TERRIER : Champion *Talavera Toddler*, the property of
Capt. H. R. Phipps of Miswell House, Tring, Herts.

THE SCOTTISH TERRIER

Origin and History.—That terriers of sorts have existed in Scotland for a considerable period is admitted, and from them have been produced four of our favourite varieties, of which that known now as the Scottish Terrier is one. Presumably the dogs from which the variety sprang bore some resemblance to their descendants, but the changes effected in the course of fifty or sixty years have been considerable. The duties of the earlier dogs being to destroy vermin, principally foxes, no one cared very much about their looks, the main consideration being, quite rightly, how they were able to do their work. That, however, would not do for show dogs which must all approach a certain ideal.

If you read about Scottish Terriers in some of the older publications that appeared towards the end of last century, you will find a good many references to strains that afterwards cropped up about 1909 when Cairn Terriers were being evolved, and the only conclusion one can reach is that all must have a certain kinship. Because the terriers we know as Scottish were first exhibited in Aberdeen, for some years they bore the name of that city, and so persistent is the use of the word that even nowadays people write to me about Aberdeen Terriers.

For the first attempts to make them known generally we must go back to 1874. These were successful enough to get classes put on at shows in 1875 and 1876, but the support given gave no promise of what was to come later. A photograph of *Roger Rough*, born 1876, whose name appears in many subsequent pedigrees, shows the stamp of terrier that was then favoured. On the whole, I should say that this dog looked more like a Cairn than a Scottie, though his expression is not bad. The head was much shorter than those we now expect to see. Within a few years progress was so rapid that classes filled well, and thence onwards Scottish Terriers have been an integral part of British life, contributing substantial entries to shows and finding a place in many homes. There are many reasons why they should be liked as companion dogs, one of the chief, perhaps, being the strong individuality that they show. Each Scottie seems to think for himself and to seek expression for his feelings in a manner that is slightly different from that of other dogs.

When I first remember them they were largely light or dark brindle in marking, but latterly the blacks have predominated. Controversy has been aroused about this colour, some declaring that the coats of the black dogs are inferior in texture to the brindles, but I think, probably, that is more a matter of strain than anything else, though I have been told that breeding black to black persistently means the production of woolly coats, and that a brindle cross is necessary in order to maintain the harsh, wiry texture that is desired.

Mr. A. G. Cowley, who has been remarkably successful on the show bench, once wrote to me that in his opinion the bitches played the dominant part in throwing good stock, he preferring to use what we might term big, doggy matrons, having great heads, short backs, good fronts and hard coats. He is also very particular about the eye. " No eye, no terrier," is his motto. You cannot have too dark an eye, and once light eyes get into a strain it is most difficult to improve them. When Mr. W. L. McCandlish was breeding, he managed to turn out a wonderful succession of champion bitches.

Standard Description.—The general appearance of the dog is summed up in the concluding note of the Scottish Terrier Club's standard :

" The face should wear a very sharp, bright and active

expression, and the head should be carried up. The dog (owing to the shortness of his coat) should appear to be higher on the leg than he really is ; but at the same time he should look compact and possessed of great muscle in his hindquarters. In fact, a Scottish Terrier, though essentially a terrier, cannot be too powerfully put together and should be from about 9 inches to 12 inches in height."

Head.—Coming into details, a skull is required proportionately long, slightly domed and covered with short, hard hair about three-quarters of an inch long or less. It should not be quite flat, as there is a stop or drop between the eyes. The muzzle is very powerful, gradually tapering towards the nose, which should always be black and of a good size. Eyes, dark brown or hazel, small, piercing, very bright and rather sunken. Ears very small,

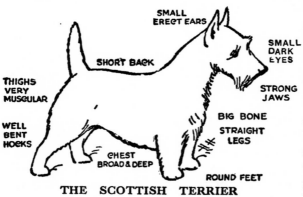

SMALL
ERECT EARS

SHORT BACK

SMALL
DARK
EYES

STRONG
JAWS

THIGHS
VERY
MUSCULAR

WELL
BENT
HOCKS

BIG BONE
STRAIGHT
LEGS

CHEST
BROAD & DEEP

ROUND FEET

THE SCOTTISH TERRIER

prick or half-prick, the former being preferable. They should be sharp-pointed and the hair should not be long but velvety. *Body*.—The neck is short, thick and muscular strongly set on sloping shoulders. Chest broad in comparison with the size of the dog and proportionately deep. Body of moderate length and rather flat-sided, well ribbed up and exceedingly strong in hindquarters. *Legs*.—Fore and hind legs short and heavy in bone, the forelegs being straight and well set on under the body. Hocks should be bent and the thighs very muscular. *Feet*.—Feet strong, small and thickly covered with short hair. *Tail*.—The tail, which should be about 7 inches long, is never docked and is carried with a slight bend, often gaily.   *Coat.*—We want a good double coat on Scottish Terriers, the under one soft, the outer very wiry, rather short and thick all over the body.   *Colour.*—This coat may be in various colours such as steel or iron-grey, black-brindle, brown-brindle, grey-brindle, black, sandy and wheaten. Sandy and wheaten are seldom seen at the present time. *Size and Weight.*—The approved size is from 15 lb. to 20 lb., the weights preferred being about 18 lb. for dogs and 16 lb. for bitches in working condition.

THE SCOTTISH TERRIER

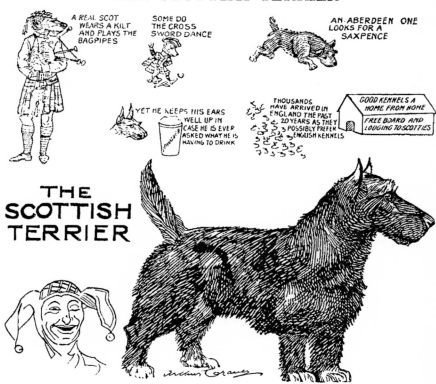

A REAL SCOT WEARS A KILT AND PLAYS THE BAGPIPES

SOME DO THE CROSS SWORD DANCE

AN ABERDEEN ONE LOOKS FOR A SAXPENCE

YET HE KEEPS HIS EARS WELL UP IN CASE HE IS EVER ASKED WHAT HE IS HAVING TO DRINK

THOUSANDS HAVE ARRIVED IN ENGLAND THE PAST 20 YEARS AS THEY POSSIBLY PREFER ENGLISH KENNELS

GOOD KENNELS A HOME FROM HOME
FREE BOARD AND LODGING TO SCOTTIES

THE SCOTTISH TERRIER

ALTHOUGH we have never been able definitely to settle the origin of the Scottish Terrier, there appears little doubt that it sprang from similar stock to the West Highland and Cairn, with possibly a mixture of the Skye terrier. During recent years this dog has been known as the Highland Terrier, then as the Aberdeen Terrier, and later on under its present-day title; yet in spite of the fact that the Kennel Club authorities some years ago decreed that they be known in future only as Scottish Terriers, we often hear them even now referred to as Aberdeens, although they are in reality very little more Aberdonian than even a Cairn.

It has taken years of thought and careful breeding to produce the present-day Scottie, as it has now broken away entirely from the Cairn-like head which it originally possessed, and the coat has changed to a marked degree, especially as regards colour. The old specimens were grey, wheaten, and brindle, while red brindle was then sought after. The black, which is now the prevailing fancy, is a " made " colour, and only secured after much trouble, although today blacks are fairly easy to breed.

The Scottie is without doubt a one-man dog. His greatest fault, if one can call it a fault, is that he is sentimental and often shy with strangers; in short, like a true Scot, only time can gain his confidence, which, when once secured, is lasting.

A Scotch Terrier should be capable of working under ground to a badger, turning a fox out of his earth, or killing a rat cleanly and quickly; in fact, he is a true terrier, and capable of doing all that a terrier should. He is handy in size, easily trained, and by no means noisy. No animal is more vigilant, and none more responsive to human treatment, as his intelligence can be developed to a high standard.

He possesses a powerful muzzle, which gradually tapers towards the nose; his skull is proportionately long and slightly domed; his body should be of moderate length, set well on short legs with heavy bone. In colour he should be steel or iron grey, black brindle, brown brindle, grey brindle, black, sandy, or wheaten. White markings are very objectionable, and from a show point of view are only allowed on the chest to a small degree.

Drawn by]

A SCOTTISH TERRIER.

[Nina Scott-Langley

These dogs have been bred for over a century. Scottish Terrier is the correct name for this breed, though it is often erroneously described as an Aberdeen Terrier.

SCOTTISH TERRIER.

Although clearly of Cairn ancestry the exact origin of the Scottish Terrier is a mystery. All that is known is that it was made, presumably, in the towns of Scotland. The breed is very popular on the Continent, the one illustrated being a prizewinner in Berlin.

befit the dog for a long day's work, severe cold or whatever hardships may befall it. Its indomitable pluck has earned for it the name "Diehard"; its coat is harsh and wiry but short, so does not pick up much dirt, and is always of a serviceable colour, ranging as it does from wheaten and sandy brindles in every variety of shade down to black. Its character is unique—only those who have had the privilege (for such it is) of owning a Scottish Terrier can fully appreciate it. As a young puppy it has an instinctive desire to please, and

A BRIGHT OUTLOOK.

Schnauzers are most intelligent and take a great interest in what goes on around them. The two shown above are obviously intrigued by something "just across the road".

Scottish Terrier.—The Scottish Terrier has for long years past held its own in the affections of the general public. Originally called the Aberdeen Terrier, it is even now sometimes asked for by that name, but the Kennel Club decreed that Scottish Terrier is its proper title, and as that it has been officially described since about 1890. The reasons for its great popularity are not far to seek. The dog is of a handy size, possessed of the strength and solidity of a big dog in the compass of a small one. It is no toy, for its vigour and hardihood and the sturdy lines on which it is built

in consequence is one of the most easily trained breeds; while so adaptable is it to circumstances of environment that it is equally satisfactory in town or country, hot climate or cold, a top-floor flat or a workman's hut, as a child's playmate, a guard of property, a sportsman's pal, the companion of an old lady, or a mere show dog.

In the last-named capacity the breed has made rapid strides. The standard of perfection has so improved that on many occasions at our larger Championship events a Scot has won Best in Show, All Breeds. There is a consistent demand for really

WIDE AWAKE.
A perky little Schnauzer puppy, the property of Mrs. Arthur Grenfell.

ette, or model may be easier if it is made to appear black is no reason for assuming that it may not be brown, grey, or any other colour. One of the almost daily trials of the average breeder is dealing with requests from people who do not know any better to supply a black puppy, just as if there was some especial merit in the colour, whereas it is actually not truly typical of the breed. Such people little know what they may be missing over texture of coat, which is a highly important feature. Invariably the other colours have better, harder, and more double coats than the blacks, whilst for a working Terrier which originated in the Highlands of Scotland, the various browns and brindles are infinitely more workmanlike and useful, with a charm all their own.

A wrong impression has got about that the head of a Scot must be big at all costs, with a lot of long hair on a square foreface, or what is technically known as "furnishing". A long head it should be, in comparison to the size of the dog, but to run away with the idea that this length should be mainly in the foreface and consist chiefly of a lot of superfluous hair is entirely wrong. Furnishing there should be in moderation, around and under the muzzle but not developed to excess, or brushed to give the face a square-ended appearance. Square at the end is precisely what a Scot's muzzle should not be. It would be well to refer to the standard of points, where attention is drawn to the outline of the nose in profile. One very erroneous belief is that a big, long foreface with lots of "whisker" on it denotes strength of jaw.

The strength of the jaw lies in the flat muscles along the cheek, and a foreface which appears longer than the skull is not only out of balance, but defeats one of the purposes for which the breed exists, that of great strength of jaw for killing

good stock of both sexes and all ages. Prices for the best specimens have soared to great heights, until it has become quite a usual practice to pay from £50 to £100 for an outstanding ten-months puppy of either sex, while full Champions of note fetch anything between £250 and £1000.

"Scottie", as it is affectionately termed by the man in the street, figures largely these days on posters, calendars, and ornaments, and these representations are largely responsible for the public's idea of what a good Scottish Terrier should be like. Though such conception is vastly better than it was, there are two mistaken beliefs on the part of the uninitiated that would be better dispelled. One concerns the colour of the dog, and the other its head.

As regards colour, exactly why the craze for blacks developed no one has ever been able to explain, but certain it is that the ordinary person setting out to buy a Scottish Terrier suffers from the peculiar delusion that black is the only correct colour. Just because the representation of a Scot in drawing, photograph, silhou-

CANINE HURDLERS.
The Schnauzers are an active breed with plenty of "go", as is evidenced by the zest and energy with which Mrs. D. McM. Kavanagh's dogs are seen taking the tennis net.

137

A SCHNAUZER IN FILMLAND.

Astrid Allwyn, a Fox Film blonde, prefers Schnauzers. She is here seen resting in the park, with Ch. "Gretchen" at her side.

HEAD OF A BLACK GIANT SCHNAUZER.
The Schnauzer is bred in three sizes, the miniature, the medium, and the giant. "Nord v. d. Hackenbergau" is a fine example of the latter variety.

139

vermin. Others may argue they have grown accustomed to seeing all the other Terrier breeds with apparently square forefaces and a great deal of whisker, and that a Scot without these features looks plain.

A correctly formed and balanced head on a dog with the right expression will never look plain, nor will it be totally devoid of "furnishing", which consists of rougher and slightly longer hair on the muzzle and eyebrows than on the rest of the face, and gives apparent depth to the foreface whilst adding to the rugged expression. Besides which, it should be realized that the correct formation of

to chin is at an acute angle to the line from eye to nose.

The oldest specialist Scottish Terrier Club was founded in 1882 or 1883, and continued as the Scottish Terrier Club (England). Their standard of points differs only very little from those of the other Scottish Terrier Clubs, and in 1933, their Jubilee year, was revised and brought up to date as follows :

STANDARD OF THE BREED, AS ADOPTED BY THE SCOTTISH TERRIER CLUB (ENG.).

GENERAL APPEARANCE.—A Scottish Terrier is a sturdy, thick-set dog of a size to get to ground,

Photo]   *[J. H. Moore.*

THREE WINNERS.

These Scottish Terrier bitches are owned by Mrs. C. M. Cross, of Elstree, Herts. They are "Gaisgill Minnie", Ch. "Gaisgill Monah", and "Gaisgill Daffodil". "Minnie" is a daughter of "Gaisgill Nicholas" out of "Gaisgill Sylvia".

the head of a Scot is different from all the other Terrier breeds. The differences lie mainly in the "stop", the expression and placement of eyes, and the typically receding profile at the mouth. The "stop" is that most essential drop just before the eyes, causing the top line of the foreface to be slightly lower than that of the skull, yet in parallel to it. The eyes should be small and almond-shaped, set deeply under the bones of the skull, and the expression is an almost indefinable mixture of keenness, quizzical seriousness, amusement, dignity, and mischief, with a strong suggestion of mystery. The slightly receding profile is one of the most characteristic features, and no Scot is ever true to type unless the line from nose

placed on short legs, alert in carriage, and suggestive of great power and activity in small compass. The head gives the impression of being long for a dog of its size. The body is covered with a close-lying, broken, rough-textured coat, and, with keen, intelligent eyes and sharp prick ears, the dog looks willing to go anywhere and do anything.

HEAD.—Without being out of proportion to the size of the dog, it should be long, the length of skull enabling it to be fairly wide and yet retain a narrow appearance. The skull is nearly flat and the cheek-bones do not protrude. There is a slight but distinct drop between skull and foreface just in front of the eye. The nose is large, and in profile the line from the nose towards the chin appears to slope backwards. The eyes are almond-shaped, dark brown, fairly wide apart and set deeply under the eyebrows. The teeth large, the upper incisors closely overlapping the lower. The ears neat, of fine texture, pointed and erect.

SHOULDERS.—The head is carried on a muscular neck of moderate length, showing quality, set into a long, sloping shoulder, the brisket well in front of the forelegs, which are straight, well boned to straight pasterns, with feet of good size and well padded, toes well arched and close knit. The chest fairly broad and hung between the forelegs, which must not be out at elbows nor placed under the body.

BODY.—The body has well-rounded ribs, which flatten to a deep chest and are carried well back. The back is proportionately short and very muscular. In general the top line of the body should be straight ; the loin muscular and deep, thus powerfully coupling the ribs to the hindquarters.

HINDQUARTERS.—Remarkably powerful for the size of the dog. Big and wide buttocks. Thighs deep and muscular, well bent at stifle. Hocks strong and well bent and neither turned inwards nor outwards. The tail, of moderate length to give a general balance to the dog, thick at the root and tapering towards the tip, is set on with an upright carriage or with a slight bend.

SIZE.—The ideally made dog in hard show condition would weigh from 17 to 21 lb.

By courtesy]   [*U. Aagaard.*
THREE BLACK RODEGAARDS.
The Scottish Terrier is almost as popular on the Continent as it is in Great Britain, and breeders across the Channel make every effort to keep the breed true to type.

COLOUR.—Black, wheaten, or brindles of any colour.

COAT.—The dog has two coats ; the undercoat short, dense, and soft ; the outer coat harsh, dense, and wiry ; the two making a weather-resisting covering to the dog.

MOVEMENT.—In spite of its short legs, the construction of the dog enables it to be very agile and active. The whole movement of the dog is smooth, easy, and straightforward, with free action at shoulder, stifle, and hock.

This standard is considered to be a description of an ideal dog, and as such should be adequate, but as a guide to the novice, it may be remarked that white as a colour is considered objectionable, except on the chest, and then only to a very small extent ; while a bad fault is any tendency to wave or curl in the coat.

The coat, with its furry and protective underjacket of wool, and its hard, flat-lying outer covering of wiry hair, is one of the most important assets. Coats are not as good and hard as they once were, owing partly to the public's demand for "whisker" already alluded to, and partly to the practice of trimming. The best-coated dogs grow only a moderate amount of whisker, and the expert trimmer can make many a poor-coated specimen seem like a good-coated one for a few weeks of its show career, but in the long run the hard coats will always prevail, for they are of slow growth,

By courtesy]   [*Mrs. A. M. Levison.*
AN INTERESTING VARIETY.
Wheaten-coloured Scottish Terriers are very rare. Mrs. A. M. Levison is the only breeder of this variety in Scandinavia. She is the owner of the famous "Heimdalhus" Kennels at Holte, Denmark, and the above are all of her breeding.

[Photo]   [J. H. Moore.

A WELL-KNOWN SCOTTISH TERRIER BREEDER.

Mrs. C. M. Cross must be classed in the front rank of breeders of the ever popular Scottie. Her famous Kennels have produced some of the finest specimens in the world, of which the above are a fair example.

Photo]   [F. R. Moore.

A CHAMPION AND ITS PUPS.

Mrs. C. M. Cross's famous Ch. "Gaitgill Motcat" is the proud mother of the adorable puppies on either side of her. They bid fair in time to enhance the name of the breed of the Gaitgills.

need less attention to keep clean and tidy, and receive their due reward, other points being equal, under judges of experience.

The words "agile", "active", "muscular" and "powerful" appear several times in the standard, and these adjectives should be borne in mind when looking for a dog of merit. Particularly should there be a great muscle, breadth and strength about the hindquarters, which give the dog great springing ability. Power and activity, short legs and substance with agility, big bone in a small dog, are all more or less contrasting terms, and the perfect Scottish Terrier, possessing these qualities with that balance and symmetry without which no animal can be said to excel, together with a long, well-proportioned head of refinement and the necessary keen expression and gameness, is not an easy dog to produce. Even the best-known specimens have always fallen short of actual perfection in some feature.

Two of the best-known Champion dogs of the breed's earliest show days were Ch. "Dundee" and Ch. "Alister". These two were half-brothers, both being sons of "Rambler". Further back than "Rambler's" sire, "Bonaccord", pedigree records do not go. "Dundee" and "Alister" made their names at stud as well as on the bench, for they became famous sires, and, strange though it may seem, there is absolutely no other male line in the breed—in other words, every Scot of to-day is descended from either Ch. "Alister" or Ch. "Dundee".

Directly descended in tail male from "Alister" came "Heather Prince", a dog which sired five Champions and proved the main link by which this line was carried on. The name of perhaps his best-known son, Ch. "Heather Bob", figured more than any other sire in the pedigrees of subsequent winners, though he only begat three Champions. He was one of the greatest show dogs of his day

(about 1900). Later in the same male line came "Claymore" and his famous son, Ch. "Claymore Defender". The latter sired three Champions, among them being the—at that period (1910)—sensational Ch. "Bapton Norman". "Norman" created something of a stir, because he conformed more nearly to the ideal breeders had set themselves to attain in the direction of straight fronts and shorter bodies, than many of his competitors. He also excelled in smallness of ears, and alertness of carriage, but his critics faulted him for lack of bone. He sired seven Champions, but curiously enough it was not through him, but through his brother, "Bapton Noble", that the "Alister" male line was carried on to further triumphs. To Ch. "Laindon Luminary", born in 1915, and likewise sire of seven Champions, do we owe the successful continuation of this line. He was a good-coated dog of great substance and good length and type of head, very low swung, with heavy bone, and was up to size. His hindquarters were not his strong point. In tail male descent from him came Ch. "Heather Necessity", famed throughout the world as a winner of a record number of Championships in the breed, one of the few to which the honour of going Best in Show All Breeds has fallen, and the sire of no fewer than fifteen British Champions.

Another branch of the "Alister" line, descending direct from Ch. "Laindon Luminary" by another route, is that branch notable for the production of Ch. "Albourne Barty", one of the most successful sires of all times. "Barty" was born in 1925, became a full Champion two years later, was a great show dog, and sired seven Champions. But in addition to this, his influence as a sire of bitches which in their turn bred outstanding winners was of immense value. As regards his own merits, his ribs, loin, coat, bone and feet left little to be

Photo]   [S. H. Benson.
THE SCOTTISH TERRIER.
Bred by Mr. W. Singleton from Ch. "Heather Fashion Hint" ex Ch. "Walsing Whisper", "Walsing Wallet" was born in 1933. In 1934 it was exhibited by Mr. Robert Chapman and became a Champion.

144

desired. He was very powerfully put together, yet combined with this symmetry and activity and was the right size. The only points in which he failed somewhat were eye, skull and expression.

To revert to Ch. "Dundee", the founder of the only other male line in the breed. In direct male descent from him came one of the most prepotent of all sires, "Seafield Rascal". In times when Championship shows were far less frequent (about 1898 to 1904) "Seafield Rascal" sired six Champions, and with the aid of his many descendants played a big part in the development of the breed. In male descent from him came another sire of great prepotency for good. This was "Laindon Lockhart", a dog which was considered slightly over-big but possessed of great character and most of the essential attributes. "Lockhart" and his sons carried on the Dundee line to many notable sires of more modern times, the most successful of which include "Laindon Lore", Ch. "Albourne Beetle", Ch. "Bobbie Burcott", "Waterford Wagtail", "Abertay Sport", and Ch. "Tweburn Clincher".

It must not be assumed that the few names given are those of the best show dogs of the past; they represent the more important links in the male lines of the breed.

During a period of fifty-odd years there were two hundred Champions, both dogs and bitches, but only a small proportion of these attained marked success as breeders. Often the most impressive sires and dams have not been Champions themselves.

Turning to the female side, which in the opinion of many is by far the most important, we find that thirty-nine different "families" have accounted for producing these two hundred Champions; a "family", of course, meaning a bitch and her female descendants, her daughter, daughter's daughter, and so on. Every male dog, of course, comes from one

By courtesy]   *[O. Aagaard.*

THREE RODEGAARDS.

The Rodegaard Kennels of Horve, Denmark, owned by the Misses Ellinor Wittrock and Olga Aagaard, specialize in the breeding of Scottish and Lakeland Terriers (derived from British stock) and Great Danes.

family or another, but does not form part of that family; just as every bitch is one or other of the male lines, but does not form part of a male line.

The largest and most successful family in the production of winners is that descended in tail female from a bitch called "Splinter II", and classified as Family 1. Sixty-one out of two hundred Champions trace their female descent to Family 1, and it is worthy of note in passing that what may be termed the most influential of the successful bitches in this family came from blending the family with the "Dundee" male line, and not with the "Alister" line, Ch. "Seafield Beauty", and of more recent years, Albourne "Annie Laurie", being outstanding examples. "Beauty" was sired by "Seafield Rascal", and "Annie Laurie" was by "Albourne McAndy", a red-brindle dog in tail male descent from Ch. "Albourne Beetle". "Seafield Beauty" started off a sequence of four Champion bitches in tail female (Ch. "Ems Cosmetic", Ch. "Ems Vanity", and Ch. "Ems Mode"), and this branch of the family was later particularly rich in Champions, both male and female, including the great Ch. "Albourne Barty". "Annie Laurie" beat all producing records in the breed by becoming the dam of six British Champions. Obviously the number of progeny a bitch can have in a lifetime, as compared to a dog, is very limited, and it is only the few exceptions which have the rare power to breed good ones in every litter.

The family next in importance, as having produced twenty-three Champions, is Family 4, that founded by a bitch named "Old Nell" (origin unknown). Its first Champion was a bitch, Ch. "Ashey Nettle", bred in 1884, and its latest three were the brothers Ch. "Rouken Rogue" and Ch. "Tremont", which attained their final honours in 1932 and 1933, and the bitch Ch. "Brimstone Belle", which qualified in 1933.

145

"WISTFUL JILL".

An appealing pen-and-ink sketch of a charming pet, specially drawn for this Work by E. G. Chapman.

A HEIMDALHUS GROUP

Mrs. Alf Murrel Levison with some of her famous Scottish Terriers. The wheaten specimen makes a striking contrast in the midst of its dark-hued consin.

Nineteen Champions come from Family 3, including such notable dogs as Ch. "Gair", Ch. "Heworth Bantock", the wheaten-coloured Ch. "Ems Morning Nip", Ch. "Albourne Beetle", and Ch. "Broxton Buckel", and such bitches as Ch. "Glory", Ch. "Laindon Ledwine", and Ch. "Ornsay June" among others. It is noticeable that two-thirds were sired by "Alister" line dogs, not "Dundee".

The breed's earliest Champion, Ch. "Syringa" (pedigree unknown), founded the group known as Family 6. She was born about 1877, but no further Champions emanated from this bitch line until 1920, when Ch. "Bellstane Lassie" appeared on the scene and revived the family fortunes. She was one of a famous litter, by a son of Ch. "Bapton Norman" out of "Meadow Lass", all of which made their names at the stud and on the bench. "Lassie" her-

little group is worthy of notice, for it involved close in-breeding similar to that practised with the majority of the earlier successful pillars of the breed. "Madre Tordo", mated to the unrelated "Brockwell Jack", bred the bitch "Scricciolo". The latter was mated to "Laindon Lore", a dog from the same male blood as "Brockwell Jack", and produced the well-known sire "Waterford Wagtail". "Scricciolo" was next mated to her son "Waterford Wagtail", and as a result bred the two bitch Champions Ch. "Tattenham Treat" and Ch. "Tattenham Treasure". From these two (more particularly from "Treasure") descended a group of bitches of valuable prepotency.

The pillars of the breed in the past were much more in-bred than those of more recent times. This was possibly due to the fact that good material was scarce, and that transit of

Photo]   [Fall.

CH. "ROSE MARIE OF ROOKES".

This Scottish Terrier, bred in 1931 by Mr. J. Chapman, was exhibited by Mrs. D. J. Sharpe. "Rose Marie" is a brindle and was sired by Ch. "Heather Necessity".

-self became the dam of three Champions, and from her in tail female descends Ch. "Ortley Elegance", in her turn the progenitress of three Champion bitches, Ch. "Ortley Carmen", Ch. "Ortley Patience", and Ch. "Ortley Angela".

Family 2 comes next in importance, having produced twelve Champions, and these have been mainly the descendants in tail female from the well-known groups of bitches of the Tattenham prefix. The method of founding this influential

the bitch to the stud dog was not so easy; or it may have been because breeders preferred to concentrate on intensifying the good qualities of what they already had rather than risk introducing different blood with the possibility of inheriting failings their own stock did not possess. A study of the earlier pedigrees provides the present-day breeder with much food for thought.

To be successful, in-breeding should only be resorted to where the individuals used are

CH. "SCOTIA GENEROUS GIFT".

Mrs. Cecil Barber's Kennel prefix is "Scotia". The above shows her beautiful little dog "Generous Gift", a great credit to her Kennel.

quite sound mentally and physically. Naturally the effect is to intensify the characteristics of both parents and their antecedents, and if any failings are present, these will be intensified just as much as the virtues.

As a word of warning, whatever the modern breeder may set out to produce, may he above all things retain the self-possessed temperament, the characteristic expression, and the active hardihood so essential to the breed.

There are five specialist Clubs for the breed in Great Britain: the Durham and Northumberland S.T.C.; the Northern Counties S.T.C.; the North of England S.T.C.; the S.T.C. England; and the S.T.C. Scotland. The two last named are the oldest established, and both hold annual Championship shows.

A diet of plain meat, reduced in amount, is indicated; a purge must be given and exercise afforded. It would be as well to obtain a correct diagnosis from a veterinary surgeon before doing anything else in the matter, as the condition may not be eczema.

Inflammation of the scrotum may arise from blows, and in such a case not only may the scrotal sac be swollen, but the testicles also may be involved. No skin lesions, such as have been described for scrotal eczema, would be present in inflammation due to contusion. For this malady, liberal bathing with hot water would be beneficial, and the dog must be rested. Occasionally one encounters cases of lacerated scrotum due to bites or barbed-wire, etc., but such accidents are comparatively rare. Unless the testicle itself is injured, scrotal wounds heal up quite well. (*See* TESTICLE.)

Even less frequently one may see dogs with hydrocele, which is a collection of serous fluid in the scrotum, causing the latter to assume much greater size and thus come into greater prominence. The sac feels doughy and fluctuates upon digital pressure. Extreme caution must be exercised in diagnosis to distinguish hydrocele from sarcocele (which is a collective name for all kinds of swellings, cysts or tumours of the testicle) and from scrotal hernia. A mistake in diagnosis, followed by inappropriate treatment, may cause the animal's death. The matter is essentially surgical and must be left to an expert.

CH. "GREYLING OF ROOKES".

Mrs. D. J. Sharpe's "Greyling" was sired by Ch. "Masterpiece of Rookes"; the mother was "Heather Ideal". This dog was born in 1932 and became a Champion in 1934.

149

Photo] [*Fall.*

THREE CHAMPIONS.

These Scottish Terriers are all Champions, and were bred by Mr. C. Bennet, who owns a leading Kennel. On the left is "Ortley Elegance" in the centre "Ortley Carman", and on the right "Ortley Angela".

[A. Robinson

"MALDEN DHU" AND FAMILY

"Malden Dhu" is a Scottish Terrier stud dog owned by Dr. and Mrs. M. E. Gordon, of Templecombe, Somersetshire. "Dhu" posited is seen with some of his legitimate offspring.

[Photo]

151

Photo]

TWO "ORTLEYS".

[Fall.

Ch. "Ortley Pilot" is the well-known stud dog at Sutton Ings, Hull, owned by Mr. Conrad Bremer. "Pilot" is a son of Ch. "Heather Ambition" and "Ortley Donna Clara".

Photo]   [R. Robinson.

POPULAR YOUNGSTERS.

Capt. F. McIntyre, of Churt, Halewell, is an enthusiastic breeder
of Scottish Terriers.   The above two charming youngsters are
members of his Kennels.

Photo]   [R. Robinson.

BLACK AND WHITE.

A delightful study of two Scottish breeds. The white puppies are West Highland White, the black ones Scottish Terriers.

153

Photo]   [R. Robinson.

"MALGEN DHU".

Bred by Miss A. D. Trotter, Ch. "Sandheys Sentry" was the sire, and "Langrange Trixie" the dam of "Malgen Dhu", which was born in 1930, and is owned by Dr. and Mrs. Ganlen.

Photo]   [R. Robinson.

MISS RUTTER'S PUPPY.

An appealing study of a young Scottie in the last phase of puppyhood, when a young dog begins to acquire a more serious outlook on life.

154

[Walter Gorees.

TAKING IT EASY.

The above two Scottish Terrier bitches, in an advanced stage of whelping, have wisely found a spot in the sun and seem to be determined not to over-exert themselves.
May they be blessed with litters of perfect puppies!

[Photo]

155

THE SCOTTISH TERRIER   COCKTAIL OF CHALLACOMBE

THIS breed is another which can trace its origin to the Cairn Terrier. Skilful breeding produced the present type. As breeders considered the results a distinct improvement they felt a certain amount of justification in changing the name to the Scottish Terrier, especially as the new type was evolved in Scotland.

Over a century ago these dogs were known as Aberdeen Terriers, and even to-day this name is still used by some owners. Like their ancestors, they are short-bodied, rough-coated, hardy little fellows, very active and great fighters. They are very affectionate and make excellent guards, and being all black or dark brindle in colour make excellent house-dogs.

THE SCOTTISH TERRIER   LINFORD COUNT

THE SCOTTISH TERRIER   CRYSTAL and CLOVER
                                         OF CHALLACOMBE

THE SCOTTISH TERRIER

THE SCOTTISH TERRIER   A " CHALLACOMBE " SCOTTIE

THE SCOTTISH TERRIER

HEAD : Without being out of proportion to the size of the dog, it should be long, the length of skull enabling it to be fairly wide and yet retain a narrow appearance. The skull is nearly flat and the cheekbones do not protrude. There is a slight but distinct drop between skull and foreface just in front of the eye. The nose is large, and in profile the line from the nose towards the chin appears to slope backwards. The eyes are almond-shaped, dark brown, fairly wide apart and set deeply under the eyebrows. The teeth large, the upper incisors closely overlapping the lower. The ears neat, of fine texture, pointed and erect.

FOREHAND : The head is carried on a muscular neck of moderate length, showing quality, set into a long sloping shoulder, the brisket well in front of the forelegs, which are straight, well boned to straight pasterns, with feet of good size and well padded, toes well arched and close-knit. The chest fairly broad and hung between the forelegs, which must not be out at elbows nor placed under the body.

BODY : The body has well-rounded ribs, which flatten to a deep chest and are carried well back. The back is proportionately short and very muscular. In general the top line of the body should be straight ; the loin muscular and deep, thus powerfully coupling the ribs to the hindquarters.

HINDQUARTERS : Remarkably powerful for the size of the dog. Big and wide buttocks. Thighs deep and muscular, well bent at stifle. Hocks strong and well bent and neither turned inwards nor outwards. The tail, of moderate length to give a general balance to the dog, thick at the root and tapering towards the tip, is set on with an upright carriage or with a slight bend.

SIZE : The ideally-made dog in hard show condition would weigh from 17 lb. to 21 lb.

COAT : The dog has two coats ; the undercoat short, dense, and soft ; the outer coat harsh, dense, and wiry ; the two making a weather-resisting covering to the dog. COLOUR : Black, wheaten, or brindles of any colour.

MOVEMENT : In spite of its short legs, the construction of the dog enables it to be very agile and active. The whole movement of the dog is smooth, easy and straightforward, with free action at shoulder, stifle and hock.

GENERAL APPEARANCE : A Scottish Terrier is a sturdy, thickset dog of a size to get to ground, placed on short legs, alert in carriage, and suggestive of great power and activity in small compass. The head gives the impression of being long for a dog of its size. The body is covered with a close-lying, broken, rough-textured coat, and, with keen intelligent eyes and sharp prick ears, the dog looks willing to go anywhere and do anything.

CPSIA information can be obtained at www.ICGtesting.com
Printed in the USA
LVOW08*0244050515

437263LV00008B/51/P